John Dryden, Classicist and Translator

Translation and Literature

VOLUME 10, Part 1

2001

John Dryden
Classicist and Translator

Edited by
Stuart Gillespie

EDINBURGH UNIVERSITY PRESS

© Edinburgh University Press Ltd 2001
22 George Square, Edinburgh.

Typeset in Linotron Ehrhardt
by Koinonia Ltd, Bury, and
printed and bound in Great Britain
by J. W. Arrowsmith Ltd, Bristol.

A CIP record for this book is
available from the British Library.

ISBN 0 7486 1530 x
ISSN 0968-1361

Contents

Preface

This volume is both a book on Dryden and a special issue of the journal *Translation and Literature*. In both cases an anniversary is involved: the tercentenary of Dryden's death was the occasion of the conference from which the papers gathered here are drawn, while the lifespan of *Translation and Literature* is in 2001 the more modest period of a decade, or ten volumes. It is hoped that this issue will interest some regular readers of the journal in Dryden, and *vice versa*, that some readers of this issue who do not regularly encounter the journal may decide to cultivate a longer-term acquaintance with it. Full details on *Translation and Literature* can be found on its website:

http://www.eup.ed.ac.uk/newweb/journals/Translation

Thanks are due for help in editorial work to Robert Cummings; in answering queries to Kenneth Haynes, David Hopkins, Donald Mackenzie, and Nicholas Selby; and in typing to Samina Ahmed.

SFG
December 2000

Notes on Contributors

Paul Davis belongs to the Department of English at University College London. His work on seventeenth-century literature and classical translation has been published in journals including *Essays in Criticism*, *The Seventeenth Century*, and *Translation and Literature*. His current research includes a study of Dryden, Pope, and Johnson on death.

Stuart Gillespie, Reader in English Literature at Glasgow University, has been Editor of *Translation and Literature* since 1992. He has published articles and reviews on Dryden in several essay collections and in *The Cambridge Quarterly*, *Literature and Theology*, *Notes and Queries*, *RES*, *Restoration*, and the *TLS*. He is joint General Editor of the forthcoming Oxford University Press *History of Literary Translation in English*. His *Shakespeare's Books: A Dictionary of Shakespeare Sources* (Athlone Press) was published earlier this year.

Kenneth Haynes is a Professor of Classical Studies and at the Editorial Institute, Boston University. He edited the anthology *Horace in English* with Donald Carne-Ross (1996). His Penguin edition of Swinburne appeared last year. He is currently working on a translation of Martin Heidegger's *Holzwege* for Cambridge University Press.

Tom Mason teaches English at the University of Bristol. He is co-author of *The Story of Poetry* (1992), and co-editor of *The Beauties of Dryden* (1982) and *Selected Poems of Abraham Cowley* (1994). His articles and reviews on Dryden, Pope, Cowley, and Johnson have appeared in essay collections and in *The Cambridge Quarterly* and *Translation and Literature*. He is currently working on a study of the relations between poetry and the criticism of poetry in the seventeenth and eighteenth centuries.

Jan Parker is Classics Research Fellow of the Open University's Humanities Higher Education Research Group. She is an Editor of the journal *Teaching in Higher Education* and co-editor of the book series 'Teaching and Learning the Humanities in Higher Education'. She has edited *Chapman's Homer* (2000) and is author of *Dialogic Education and* *the Problematics of Translation in Homer and Greek Tragedy* (Edwin Mellen, 2001).

Felicity Rosslyn teaches in the English Department of the University of Leicester and is an Editor of *The Cambridge Quarterly*. Her work on English classicism includes an edited selection of Pope's Homer (1985). She has also published *Alexander Pope: A Literary Life* (1990) and *Tragic Plots: A New Reading from Aeschylus to Lorca* (2000).

Philip Smallwood is Professor of English at the University of Central England and author of *Modern Critics in Practice*, 1990. His writings on Augustan criticism include essays and articles on the French critics, Dryden, Pope, and Johnson. His reviews and essays on theoretical and critical-historical subjects have appeared in journals including *New Literary History* and *The Cambridge Quarterly*. He is editor of a forthcoming collection of essays *Johnson Re-Visioned* (Bucknell University Press).

Robin Sowerby is Senior Lecturer in English at Stirling University. He has published widely on Dryden's translations from the Classics, in several essay collections and notably in *Translation and Literature*. His *The Classical Legacy in English Poetry* appeared in 1994 and he is currently at work on a study of the influence of classical translations on eighteenth-century English poetry.

Charles Tomlinson, the distinguished poet and critic, edited *The Oxford Book of Verse in English Translation* in 1980. His *Poetry and Metamorphoses* (1983) also makes Dryden central in the English translating tradition. His latest volume of verse is *The Vineyard above the Sea* (1999). A collection of his essays on American subjects will be published shortly by Carcanet.

Abbreviations

Kinsley *The Poems of John Dryden*, edited by James Kinsley, 4 vols (Oxford, 1958)

Lives   *The Lives of the English Poets*, edited by George Birkbeck Hill, 3 vols (Oxford, 1905)

Poems *The Poems of John Dryden*, edited by Paul Hammond and David Hopkins, vols I–IV (London, 1995–2000)

Works *The Works of John Dryden*, edited by E. N. Hooker, H. T. Swedenberg Jr, *et al.*, 20 vols (Berkeley, 1956–)

The incomplete status of two major Dryden editions at the time of going to press leads to the use of three alternative sources of quotation and reference for Dryden texts: *Poems* where possible, *Works* for material not included in *Poems* I–IV, and Kinsley for Dryden's works 1697–1700 (principally *Fables*), not available in either *Poems* or *Works*.

Introduction

Stuart Gillespie

The papers gathered here were read at the Dryden tercentenary conference at the University of Bristol, 7–9 July 2000, organized by David Hopkins and Charles Martindale. The present volume is not intended as a complete record of the conference proceedings, since only a selection of the papers delivered is found here. Instead, by virtue of the subjects and character of the papers selected, this book constitutes a collaborative assessment of Dryden's work as translator of the classics 300 years after his death. 'Assessment' here does not mean an attempt at comprehensiveness of survey – no contribution deals, for example, with Dryden's versions of Persius – but an effort to ask difficult questions and answer them in such a way as might satisfy those (particularly non-specialists) who are not necessarily convinced about the place Dryden's translations, and to some extent translation in general, should occupy in our maps of English literature. As Felicity Rosslyn writes in her paper, 'critical consensus can always be a cover for inertia ... and even admirers may be glad of an opportunity to reassess the grounds of their enthusiasm'. The commentators published here are all concerned to make out a case, to press what they see as Dryden's claims as a classicist and translator to wider and more sustained attention – and not to preach only to the converted.

It has been decided to retain in these published versions something of the flavour of the papers as delivered by limiting the extent of after-the-event expansion and documentation. Adequate scholarly references are, of course, provided for quotations and citations, but in most cases documentation is lighter than is normal for academic articles, and several contributions are particularly pithy and provocative, conceived as a stimulus to further discussion rather than an exhaustive treatment of a subject. Some papers are, however, exceptions to these generalizations, and it has seemed best to countenance diversity rather than impose a straitjacket.

One of the striking things about hearing the papers and editing them has for me been the way they return again and again to certain decisive moments in Dryden's twenty prolific years as a translator – the highlights, for example, of the 1685 *Sylvae* volume, from Lucretius and Horace.

This perhaps suggests questions in particular about the shape of
Dryden's translating career, and implicitly challenges older assumptions
about the preeminence of the large-scale late achievements *The Works of
Virgil* and *Fables Ancient and Modern*. Equally, a number of recurrent
themes emerge distinctly across the individual contributions, in
connection with a range of different areas of Dryden's translation work:
his 'Latinity' of style and diction; the ways in which he combines
together his impressions of the various writers he reads and translates;
the pertinence of his political and religious allegiances. But if several
important questions are raised more than once, the answers are supplied
from several points of view – and indeed are by no means always the
same.

To the eight papers are added two specially commissioned review-
essays on books which, having appeared within the preceding year,
formed part of the context of the Bristol conference, and all of which are
referred to at least glancingly by contributors to the main section of this
volume. (One of them, the *Dryden Tercentenary Essays* edited by David
Hopkins and Paul Hammond, is a collection to which many of the
conference participants had contributed; some of these contributors are
not represented here at all, but others were able to offer a fresh paper on
Dryden as translator for the conference.) In these reviews as much as
anywhere is at issue the standing of Dryden's work as classicist and
translator 300 years after that work came to an end, and the critical
climate in which discussion of it is best conducted.

Why Dryden's Translations Matter

Charles Tomlinson

'Dryden', as Dr Johnson famously says in his life of the poet, 'may be properly considered as the father of English criticism'.[1] It would be gratifyingly symmetrical, but a slight exaggeration, if one could go on to claim him as 'the father of English translation' – translation of poetry, that is. Dryden is rather the most brilliant heir to that legacy of creative effort, initiated by Ben Jonson and continued throughout the seventeenth century by such poets as Fanshawe, Cowley, and Oldham, to make new the classics – Horace, Virgil, Juvenal, Lucretius – as part of the live current of English poetry.

'Make it new', in twentieth-century modernism, has often meant a violent break with the past, of the sort inaugurated by cubism and surrealism. What the seventeenth-century poets sought to achieve was a break with merely literal translation from the classics, and with that timid habit of reducing texts to moralistic tags, a mode beloved of seventeenth-century schoolmasters. English poets set out to recover as translators the kind of energies which reappeared in France, out of a vivid awareness of Martial and Horace, in the poetry of Boileau, admired by Dryden and by his own heir, Alexander Pope. Dryden appeared on the scene just as the English part of the undertaking was gathering momentum, and the artistic impetus that his own presence guaranteed 'made it new', not only for himself, but for a succeeding generation of poet-translators. As a practitioner, his prose formulations about translation carry the conviction of authority, as when in the Preface to *Sylvae* (1685) he tells us:

> a good poet is no more like himself in a dull translation, than his carcass would be to his living body. There are many who understand Greek and Latin, and yet are ignorant of their mother tongue. The proprieties and delicacies of the English are known to few; 'tis impossible even for a good wit to understand and practise them without the help of a liberal education, long reading and digesting of those few good authors we have amongst us.
>
> (*Poems*, II, 239)

I want to look at the perspective just sketched under three heads: in relation to Dryden's immediate forebears and contemporaries; in relation to Dryden's personal case and the fact that the last fifteen years of his life were chiefly dedicated to poetic translation (here I shall be touching on some of the salient themes that attract him rather than giving accounts of each text that he translated); then, finally and very briefly, Dryden in relation to the younger poets over whom he was so influential, and whose work he supervised, in a rather Ezra Poundian way, with enabling criticism. Congreve tells us, 'he was extreme ready, and gentle in his correction of the errors of any writer who thought fit to consult him'.[2] So if Dryden was the father of English criticism, he also looked on the art of translating as both a creative and a critical act: 'thus ... a man should be a nice critic in his mother tongue before he attempts to translate a foreign language'. And to cap this: 'to be a thorough translator he must be a thorough poet' (Preface to *Sylvae; Poems*, II, 240).

First, then, his poetic forebears and contemporaries, and the way in which their voices are heard in the struggle against the merely literal translation of poetry, which at the time was called 'verbal interpretation'. I'm afraid the ghost of this literalism is still with us, despite all attempts to lay it. Speak to many a classicist and mention Dryden's Horace or Pope's Homer, and you realize very quickly by their blank expression that what *they* have in mind is still something closer to Richmond Lattimore's *Iliad*, packing in all the words Homer used, regardless of the fact that the resulting idiom is one 'that never *was* on sea or land', in what Donald Carne-Ross referred to definitively thirty years ago as 'a mistaken ambition of exactness'.[3]

Samuel Johnson evidently thought this sort of thing could never happen again, when in his 'Life of Dryden' he speaks of translation of verse 'struggling for the liberty that it now enjoys'. 'Why', he goes on, 'it should find any difficulty in breaking the shackles of verbal translation [word-for-word translation, that is], which must for ever debar it from elegance, it would be difficult to conjecture, were not the power of prejudice every day observed' (*Lives*, I, 373). Now poets had long known this. We find Aurelian Townshend, who lived between 1601 and 1643, writing in 'To the Right Honorable, the Lord Cary':

> Verball Translators sticke to the bare Text,
> Sometimes so close, the Reader is perplex't,
> Finding the words, to finde the wit that sprung
> From the first writer in his native tongue.[4]

The debate was carried on by the seventeenth-century group of royalist poets, including Denham, Cowley, and Fanshawe. Sir John Denham, author of the 1656 Virgil translation *The Destruction of Troy*, cautions in the Preface to that work that, since there are 'Graces and Happinesses peculiar to every Language, which gives life and energy to the words ... whosoever offers at Verbal Translation, shall have the misfortune of that young Traveller, who lost his language abroad, and bought home no other instead of it: for the grace of the Latine will be lost by being turned into English words; and the grace of the English, by being turned into the Latin Phrase'.[5]

It was precisely in the spirit of this Preface that, when Dryden emerged as a major translator in the volume *Sylvae* of 1685, where splendid versions of Lucretius, Horace, and Theocritus appear, he wrote in his own Preface:

> Where I have taken away some of their expressions, and cut them shorter, it may possibly be on this consideration, that what was beautiful in the Greek or Latin would not appear so shining in the English: and where I have enlarged them, I desire the false critics would not always think that those thoughts are wholly mine, but that either they are secretly in the poet, or may be fairly deduced from him; or at least, if both those considerations should fail, that my own is of a piece with his, and that if he were living, and an Englishman, they are such as he would probably have written.
>
> (*Poems*, II, 237–8)

Poet–translators – think of Pound versus the sinologists and the Latin and Anglo–Saxon professors – seem to experience the need to recover this kind of confidence in almost every generation.

Sir John Denham once more. He is congratulating Sir Richard Fanshawe on the latter's 1658 version of Guarini's *Il pastor fido*:

> That servile path thou nobly dost decline
> Of tracing word by word, and line by line ...
> A new and nobler way thou dost pursue
> To make Translations and Translators too.
> They but preserve the Ashes, thou the Flame,
> True to his sense, but truer to his fame.[6]

Denham, always an acute writer on this topic, clearly means, when he sees Fanshawe's aim as 'To make Translations and Translators too', that the bold and capable translator like Fanshawe was opening a future possibility to other translators, which is exactly what Dryden was to

achieve for a younger generation of poet-translators, his own superb
Æneid preparing the way for Pope's even greater *Iliad*. Here Dryden's
Æneid set the standard, sealing the fate of one Dr Brady's subsequent
version in blank verse, which, says Johnson, 'when dragged into the
world, did not live long enough to cry' (*Lives*, I, 453).

Denham in another poem offers congratulations to that absurdly
underrated poet and translator whom Dryden calls 'the darling of my
boyhood': Abraham Cowley, whose versions of Horace and Virgil
precede and alert Dryden's own. Here is Denham on Cowley:

> Horace his wit, and *Virgil's* state,
> He did not steal, but emulate,
> And when he would like them appear,
> Their Garb, but not their Cloaths, did wear[7]

Here we have an alternative to T. S. Eliot's dictum to the effect that
great artists steal and minor ones only borrow. Not theft but emulation:
Cowley, Denham is surely implying, is penetrating in the act of translating
to the spirit of classical authors; his translations, by interpreting them
however freely, bring them to life, because Cowley does not come away
from the encounter wearing their bits and pieces, but can emulate a
civilization by his unerring sense of its style or styles. Singling out this
passage in a very different context, Donald Davie commends the razor-
edge of Denham's diction, and writes, 'it had not occurred to the reader
that the distinction between "garb" and "clothes" was so fine yet so
definite'.[8] I am reminded, too, of that comment of Ezra Pound's and his
awareness of how bad for poets other people's cast-offs can be: 'horrible
examples', he says, 'of people wearing Elizabethan old clothes ... project
from whole decades of later English and American writing'.[9]

But to return to Abraham Cowley, Dryden's admired predecessor,
who, says Dryden, 'must always be thought a great Poet' (Kinsley, IV,
1452). Milton, Pope, Johnson all concurred in this judgement. Our own
century has thought otherwise, perhaps because some of Cowley's most
brilliant work is in the form of translation, an art which has only recently
begun to receive its grudging due. Even at the age of thirteen, Cowley,
a Mozartian wonder, had found his way to that side of Horace which was
to appeal so strongly to poets who had experienced the Civil War and its
aftermath, or who, like Cowley later on, were disappointed courtiers
wishing to withdraw to a world of personal probity and quiet self-
possession, away from the duplicity and obsequiousness of court circles.
Johnson, in his 'Life of Dryden', registers the corruption that such a
milieu involved for the poet when he comments on one of Dryden's royal

dedications that it is 'in a strain of flattery which disgraces genius, and which it was wonderful that any man that knew the meaning of his own words could use without self-detestation' (*Lives*, I, 359).

The thirteen-year-old Cowley – both prematurely and ironically, in view of the subsequent effect of the Civil War on his life and fortunes – was already responding to that vein of Horace which appealed to other subsequently disabused royalists, rewarded late if at all for their adherence to the Stuart cause, or, like Dryden, in his post as Poet Laureate and Historiographer Royal, with salary unpaid and often up to two years in arrears. The boy Cowley responded to Horace with lines that imitate and wear the garb of the Roman poet in his search for ease of mind and an inner contentment at having lived fully and true to oneself:

> I would not fear nor wish my fate,
>   But boldly say each night,
> To morrow let my Sun his beams display,
> Or in clouds hide them; I have liv'd to Day.[10]

This conclusion, says Cowley, 'is taken out of *Horace*'. These characters, he adds, were early engraved within him: 'They were like Letters cut into the Bark of a young Tree, which with the Tree still grow proportionably.' Cowley's beautiful image says much about the effects of early learning, and of learning the right thing, on the mind and memory of the individual. It says much about teaching by way of the classical languages, and daily translation practice which was the mode throughout English grammar schools, and specifically at Westminster School where Jonson, Cowley, and Dryden were all pupils at different periods.

Cowley was to continue not only to translate Horace, but to imitate him in later life, writing: 'I am not so much enamoured of the *Name Translator*, as not to wish to be *Something Better*, though it want yet a Name.'[11] One result of this approach was his masterpiece, an imitation of Horace's tale of the town and country mouse whose lightness of tone carries with ease the moral theme of being true to oneself. The country mouse offers his town guest something from the uncontaminated bounty of nature:

> Fitches and Beans, Peason, and Oats, and Wheat,
> And a large Chesnut, the delicious meat
> Which *Jove* himself, were he a Mouse, would eat.
>   (Cowley, II, 414)

But the visiting Londoner has his mind on less homely fare, and urges his rural friend

> [to] taste the generous Lux'ury of the Court,
> Where all the Mice of quality resort
> (Cowley, II, 415)

Cowley, along with his poetic contemporaries and in tune with Horace, keeps reverting to the idea of rural self-sufficiency. Here Virgil enters the picture with Cowley's translation of *Georgics* II:

> O happy, (if his Happiness he knows)
> The Country Swain, on whom kind Heav'n bestows
> At home all Riches that wise Nature needs;
> Whom the just earth with easie plenty feeds.
> (Cowley, II, 409)

Cowley also renders a similar dream of sufficiency from Horace's Epode II:

> Happy the Man whom bounteous Gods allow
> With his own Hands Paternal Grounds to plough!
> Like the first golden Mortals Happy he
> From Business and the cares of Money free!
> (Cowley, II, 412)

These Virgilian sentiments are undercut at the conclusion of Horace's poem, where we see that they are just the daydreams of a usurer who soon hastens back to pecuniary transactions. Cowley omits this final bit of the original, because the same dream he had found in Virgil's *Georgics* evidently appealed to him so deeply. Dryden, too, speaks of 'all the perfection that can be expected in a Poem written by the greatest Poet in the Flower of his Age' (*Works*, V, 153), in referring not to Virgil's *Æneid* but to the *Georgics* themselves, his own outstanding triumph of translation from the Virgilian canon. Both Cowley and Dryden are warmly attracted to that figure of the morally upright agriculturalist as against the thankless court milieu they had known. The image of the Virgilian small farmer would have had its obvious resonance, too, for Latin-reading country gentlemen in Civil War and post-Civil War England. Despite Virgil's directions about when to plough or how to handle your bees, there was also a kind of mythic overplus about this figure, something transferable from the Roman to the English scene. He isn't, for all the apparent basis of realism in the poem, an entirely realistic character. As Alistair Elliot tells us in his edition of Dryden's *Georgics* plus Latin text: 'He is a richer, vaguer figure, more like the universal farming ancestor, the greater and greater, grander and grander grandfather who lived when Adam delved (if not Eve).'[12]

The desire for moral self-sufficiency clearly played a main role in the career of Dryden, to whom I now turn at the time of his crisis of the mid-1670s onwards, as he grows more and more conscious of wasted powers and of the artistic futility of his attempt to live by serving up to the London theatre the plays that would be box office successes. Two names of friends appear in the context of Dryden's energetic transference of interest from the theatre to translation: Jacob Tonson, the publisher, and Wentworth Dillon, Earl of Roscommon, to whose *An Essay on Translated Verse* of 1684 Dryden wrote a Preface, also in verse, in which he sees English poetry and, by implication, translation of poetry into English, as making our own literature equal to the classics, so that the poets – 'the few beloved by Jove' – will

> On equal terms with ancient wit engage,
> Nor mighty Homer fear, nor sacred Virgil's page:
> Our English palace opens wide in state,
> And without stooping they may pass the gate.
>
> *(Poems*, II, 222)

With his customary incisiveness, Donald Carne-Ross has argued against the translator setting up English 'on equal terms with ancient wit', and he insists that a translator ought to leave signs of the irreducibly foreign element in texts from other languages, as Ezra Pound does in translating the Confucian Odes. I find the expression of this idea persuasive, though I don't think I would accuse Dryden, as Carne-Ross does, of 'a certain provincial arrogance', of '[setting] over the door of the house of translation a sign announcing, "English only spoken. No foreign tricks allowed here."'[13] This charge of provincialism perhaps seems somewhat unfair, when, as we know, translations in the seventeenth century were frequently read side-by-side with the Latin originals, so that the reader could compare and contrast. As for 'foreign tricks', Dryden and his contemporaries were Latinists from a tender age, so 'English only spoken' would have seemed a provincial attitude to them also. This overriding desire to get things into English, chiefly from Latin but also from Greek, is surely a historic attempt morally to reinforce English from classical sources – sources whose profound literary insights could be educative and sustaining – at a time when English culture was suffering from the terrible schisms of the Civil War and afterwards. If you could engage 'on equal terms with ancient wit', then maybe all was not lost, and England and English could draw on and realign fractured potential.

One of the manifestations of Dryden's exceptional linguistic awareness is the way he dramatizes the explosive meeting of Saxon monosyllables with the superior melopoeia (as he saw it) of polysyllabic Latin. His Saxon monosyllables actually emphasize the barbarism which stalks the classical text. The foreign element – the Latin – is brought out in Dryden's Ovid and Virgil in a head–on collision with a decidedly atavistic English. Eric Griffiths gives an excellent example of this,[14] where Æneas sees the ghost of Hector, and Greco-Latin is confronted by Anglo-Saxon:

> Such as he was, when, by *Pelides* slain,
> *Thessalian* Coursers drag'd him o're the Plain.
> Swoln were his Feet, as when the Thongs were thrust
> Through the bor'd holes, his Body black with dust
> (*Æneis*, II, 354–7; *Works*, V, 390)

But let us return to the Earl of Roscommon and that *Essay on Translated Verse*.

Dryden's sympathy for Roscommon's *Essay* must have been deepened by the latter's sense that translation is not just another piece of literary business, and that for the finest translation to take place there must be an affinity between translator and original author. Playing with the Pythagorean idea of the transmigration of souls, Dryden came to feel that, just as Milton had inherited the soul of Spenser, and Spenser imagined 'that the Soul of *Chaucer* was transfus'd into his Body', he, John Dryden, also had 'a Soul congenial to [Chaucer's]' (Preface to *Fables*; Kinsley, IV, 1445). In translating that poet, as he was to do in his final book, *Fables*, Dryden half-jestingly implies that the transmigration of souls (metempsychosis) is at work especially in the act of translation, so that you had better choose a text where you are the soul-mate or perhaps the transfus'd soul of the previous author. This ability to identify oneself with one's original is a theme that evidently attracted him to Roscommon's poem, and especially, one imagines, to these lines of baroque sprezzatura:

> Then, seek a *Poet* who *your* way do's bend,
> And chuse an *Author* as you chuse a *Friend*.
> United by this *Sympathetick Bond*,
> You grow *Familiar*, *Intimate* and Fond;

> Your *thoughts*, your *Words*, your *Stiles*, your *Souls* agree,
> No longer his *Interpreter*, but *He.*[15]

There is a certain poetic licence in Roscommon's sprezzatura. After all, if you *become* the man you are translating, you abolish that linguistic space between you within which the creativity of translating can occur.

We get a glimpse from Roscommon of the seventeenth-century way of translating, using every hint you can from previous translators and commentators. Dryden, when he came to translate Virgil, used up to nine previous editions and their commentaries. Thus Roscommon writes:

> Take pains the *genuine* Meaning to explore,
> There *Sweat*, there *Strain*, tug the laborious *Oar*:
> Search *ev'ry Comment*, that your Care can find,
> Some here, some there, may hit the Poets *Mind*[16]

So what Roscommon is offering is not translation theory, but a practical guide on how to do it, to which Dryden, as a practitioner, could respond.

Scholars have discovered more for us of another relationship that shored up Dryden in his years of difficulty, that with Jacob Tonson, an emerging publisher who was to become the Faber & Faber of his day and the leading publisher of translated literature. Tonson was the effective force making possible in financial terms this renaissance of the classics in English, combining in his list an impressive range of both prose and verse in translation, together with editions of the chief English poets, including Milton, Cowley, Shakespeare, and Spenser, not to mention Tonson's miscellanies in which much contemporary work, including Dryden's, appeared. Without Tonson, Dryden would not so easily have rescued himself either financially or morally from his dilemma, though, time and again, financial necessity was to drive him back into the theatre.

At the height of his moral crisis, Dryden was drawn more and more into translation, not only as a way of making a living, but also as a means of self-exploration. Concerning the passages of bombast in his plays he would come to say, 'I knew they were bad enough to please, even when I writ them.'[17] And in his ode on the death of the youthful poet, Anne Killigrew, we hear the unmistakable note of self-disgust that had undermined hopes of a Horatian quiet mind:

> O gracious God, how far have we
> Profaned thy heavenly gift of poesy!
> Made prostitute and profligate the Muse,
> Debased to each obscene and impious use,

> Whose harmony was first ordained above
> For tongues of angels, and for hymns of love!
> O wretched we, why were we hurried down
>   This lubric and adulterate age
> (Nay added fat pollutions of our own)
> T' increase the steaming ordures of the stage?
>   (56–65; *Poems*, III, 9–10)

Dryden, at this time, seems to be passing in review the terms of his moral existence. Made Poet Laureate at the age of thirty-seven, here he was beyond the middle years of his life, the author of some powerful poems, but guilty of the unevenness of which Johnson complains. He was coming gradually to see the unparalleled achievement of Milton's *Paradise Lost* as a living reproach to him. 'This man', he is reported as saying, 'cutts us all out, and the ancients too'.[18]

The death of a young compeer of Dryden's, the poet and translator John Oldham, also deeply affected the former's sense of last things and lost opportunities:

> Farewell, too little and too lately known,
> Whom I began to think and call my own;
> For sure our souls were near allied, and thine
> Cast in the same poetic mould with mine.
> One common note on either lyre did strike,
> And knaves and fools we both abhorred alike:
> To the same goal did both our studies drive,
> The last set out the soonest did arrive.
>   (1–8; *Poems*, II, 230)

In short, the youthful genius of John Oldham had led him, ahead of Dryden, first to satire, but also to see how verse translation could be a major undertaking for the poet. Oldham had already, by the time of his early death at the age of thirty in 1683, translated into lively English substantial quantities of Horace, Juvenal, and (among the moderns) Boileau.

Oldham's central influence had been Abraham Cowley, from whose favourite types of translation he had learned much – the two types defined by Dryden as 'paraphrase, or translation with latitude, where the author is kept in view by the translator, so as never to be lost, but his words are not so strictly followed as his sense and that too is admitted to be amplified, but not altered'. The second type was 'imitation, where the translator (if now he has not lost that name) assumes the liberty not only to vary from the words and sense, but to forsake them both as he sees occasion; and taking only some general hints from the original, to run division on the ground-work as he pleases' (Preface to *Ovid's Epistles*; *Poems*, I, 384–5). Dryden's words bring to mind those of Cowley we have already heard: 'I am not so enamoured of the Name Translator, as not to want to be Something Better.' Following Cowley's hint, Oldham produces one of the masterpieces of that Horatian-Virgilian tradition that Dryden was to extend, and that I have touched upon, the 'Beatus Ille'. The blessings this time, in Horace's Ode 31, Book I, belong to the poet, defined in terms of the basic bounties of nature, 'olives, succories and emollient mallows'. The things Horace doesn't want are given as the names of commodities to be had from far around the Mediterranean and the East. These are all changed by Oldham as he '[runs] division on the ground-work as he pleases' and Horace's rejected exotica are made English:

> What does the Poet's modest Wish require?
> What Boon does he of gracious Heav'n desire?
> Not the large Crops of *Esham*'s goodly Soil,
> Which tire the Mower's and the Reaper's toil:
> Not the soft Flocks, on hilly *Cotswold* fed,
> Nor *Lemster* Fields with living Fleeces clad[19]

No wonder, in the light of work like this, that Dryden found an exceptional poet to mourn, a poet whose quality was to be saluted by Pope and whose imitation of Juvenal's Satire III supplied the ground-work for Samuel Johnson's own imitation of Juvenal in his poem *London*. Paul Hammond's admirable book *John Oldham and the Renewal of Classical Culture* speaks of the 'urgent thinking that takes place as Oldham composes his translations that establishes their independence from their models', and he underlines for us their 'abiding value, and their function as a critical preparation for the work of Dryden, Pope and Johnson'.[20] Towards the end of Oldham's imitation of Horace's Ode I.31, after a rich evocation of the copious variety supplied by the natural world, we come to the wish for 'sound Health, impair'd by no Disease' (38) – a line which must have carried personal meaning for the consumptive Oldham. Hammond comments: 'What happens in Dryden's versions of Horace, and ... in Oldham's, is that the poet evokes the sensuous delights of life with a greater zest and discrimination because he is reappraising their value in a world menaced by Fortune and death.'

Dryden's elegy for Oldham tolls the bell of an inner significance for Dryden himself, as he passes through the critical years that see the culmination of his disgust with crown and theatre, as he perhaps reflects

on other deaths of major poets – Cowley, Rochester, Milton. There is a
dramatic rightness and a montage swiftness for the reader of a collected
edition of Dryden in that, turning the page of Dryden's elegy for his
friend, one comes immediately upon the title *Sylvae* (1685), that
wonderfully compact collection of poems in which Dryden emerges in
his mid-fifties as the finest poetic translator of his age. *Sylvae* opens with
passages translated from Lucretius, and these replicate once more that
sense of the copiousness of life in the lovely evocation of Venus, 'Delight
of human kind and gods above, / Parent of Rome, propitious Queen of
love' (*Poems*, II, 308), and then follows *Against the Fear of Death*, that
amazing and exultant celebration of death, not as the way aloft, as one
might have expected from a Christian and a Catholic, but as the end of
all things:

> We, who are dead and gone, shall bear no part
> In all the pleasures, nor shall feel the smart ...
> And last, suppose great Nature's voice should call
> To thee, or me, or any of us all ...
> If all the bounteous blessings I could give   ⎫
> Thou hast enjoyed, if thou hast known to live,   ⎬
> And pleasure not leaked through thee like a sieve, ⎭
> Why dost thou not give thanks as at a plenteous feast,
> Crammed to the throat with life, and rise and take thy rest?
>   (27–8, 121–2, 127–31; *Poems*, II, 318, 322)

The way Dryden edits his chosen fragments of translation involves us
in a world of mighty opposites: love and death, the love that is delightful,
the love that is ferocious, the love that combines both pleasure and
desperation issuing in a sort of philosophical comedy – as in (from
Lucretius still):

> Our hands pull nothing from the parts they strain,
> But wander o'er the lovely limbs in vain:
> Nor when the youthful pair more closely join,
> When hands in hands they lock, and thighs in thighs they twine,
> Just in the raging foam of full desire,
> When both press on, both murmur, both expire,
> They gripe, they squeeze, their humid tongues they dart,
> As each would force their way to t' others heart—
> In vain; they only cruise about the coast,
> For bodies cannot pierce, nor be in bodies lost
>   (69–78; *Poems*, II, 335–6)

One sees here what Johnson meant when he said that Dryden was not one of the gentle bosoms, and that love appealed to him 'in its turbulent effervescence with some other desires' (*Lives*, I, 458). But Lucretius also has his Horatian side, and Dryden warms to this too, translating a passage that contains Horace's image of the boat moving safely close to the shore, along with thoughts of the quiet mind sufficient unto itself:

> To virtue's heights, with wisdom well supplied,
> And all the magazines of learning fortified ...
> A soul serene, a body void of pain.
> So little this corporeal frame requires,
> So bounded are our natural desires
> (*Poems*, II, 312, 313–14)

The equanimity of this is of a piece with the equanimity of Dryden's finest Horatian translation, Ode III.29, where with Horace he urges his aristocratic friend to lay aside 'the busy pageantry / That wise men scorn, and fools adore' (19–20). We are back with that side of Horace the boy Cowley seized on, but for Dryden Horace's lesson comes home with all the force of adult life and years of political and personal vicissitude:

> Happy the man, and happy he alone,
> He who can call to day his own:
> He who secure within can say,
> 'Tomorrow do thy worst, for I have lived today ...'
>
> Fortune, that with malicious joy
> Does Man her slave oppress,
> Proud of her office to destroy
> Is seldome pleased to bless ...
> I can enjoy her while she's kind,
> But when she dances in the wind
> And shakes her wings, and will not stay,
> I puff the prostitute away ...
> (65–6, 73–6, 81–4; *Poems*, II, 374–5)

And we end the poem in that safe Horatian boat, 'Contemning all the blustering roar', 'Within some little winding creek, / And see the storm ashore'.

From the violence of parts of his Lucretius to the balance of his Horace may seem a fair stride. But 'without contraries is no progression', and Blake's aphorism expresses for us the apparent anomaly of Dryden and his mighty opposites: here is a Royalist who satirizes kings, a

Catholic who despises priests, a lover of the quiet life and the quiet mind
who delights in the vivid description of fire, flood, battle, and sex, and
who uses translation to extend his range with these very subjects. Poets
are often the least conventionally accountable of creatures, like small
children, 'Their aim as much the wonder as the cause', as one of them
writes. Dryden can even wonder at the sleazily phallocentric Charles II,
thinly disguised as King David in *Absalom and Achitophel*:

> When Nature prompted, and no law denied
> Promiscuous use of concubine and bride;
> Then Israel's monarch, after heaven's own heart,
> His vigorous warmth did variously impart
> To wives and slaves: and wide as his command
> Scattered his maker's image through the land.
>   (5–10; *Poems*, I, 455)

When Dryden comes to translate Juvenal's Satire VI (published in 1693)
there is something of he same 'gust', as he calls it, in his treatment of the
Empress Messalina. Challenged, he might reply to the question of why
he chose to wonder at her, as he did to that of why he translated the love
passages in Lucretius: 'I own it pleased me.'[21] Messalina, like Horace's
Cleopatra, is a creature to be marvelled at, a strange monster. Yet if
anybody ever believed Juvenal was simply an improving writer, chiefly
intent on exposing and curbing the ills of Rome, Dryden's version soon
gets rid of that pious myth, with his astonished and astonishing portrait
of this woman who slips out of the royal bed and takes on the customers
of a brothel:

> At length, when friendly darkness is expired,
> And every strumpet from her cell retired,
> She lags behind, and, lingering at the gate,
> With a repining sigh submits to fate;
> All filth without, and all a-fire within,
> Tired with the toil, unsated with the sin.
> Old Caesar's bed the modest matron seeks,
> The steam of lamps still hanging on her cheeks
> In ropy smut; thus foul, and thus bedight,
> She brings him back the product of the night.
>   (180–9; *Poems*, IV, 58)

Like King David, Messalina is as much a cosmic force as a human being,
and it is this obsession with cosmic forces, swirling around the precariously

human, that makes Dryden the perfect translator of Virgil's *Georgics*, with their lynxes, wolves, stags, and horses, turned frantic by the seasonal force of spring. The same is true of his versions from Ovid's *Metamorphoses*, and its series of instinctually driven characters, its violent not-to-be-resisted transformations, its dwelling on murder, incest, lust. The philosophical side of Ovid, the 'Pythagorean philosophy', also mirrors Lucretius' sense of 'this ever-changing frame's decay, / New things to come, and old to pass away' (*Poems*, II, 324), translated by Dryden previously.

Dryden had to put to one side the Ovid versions he had been working on for the young publisher, Jacob Tonson, to undertake the more lucrative complete Virgil, and some of these Ovidian pieces were to turn up in his final and greatest volume – largely one of translations – *Fables Ancient and Modern*, published just two months before his death in 1700. I have time only to mention in passing the superb rendering of Ovid's first book plus assorted metamorphoses that came out in Dryden's *Examen Poeticum* ('A Swarm of Poems') of 1693.

It would be foolish at this point to embark on a blow-by-blow account of Dryden's *Æneid*. I have already mentioned the masterly *Georgics* with which he began his work on the Virgilian canon. There is a sense of the human involvement in natural and animal processes here. This sense parallels a theme that had drawn Dryden to the work he had to defer, namely Ovid's *Metamorphoses*. His dealings with the *Metamorphoses* and the way he reaches into the future via his stylistic influence on those younger poets who were to complete the project, must now lead me towards my conclusion.

Like the *Georgics*, the *Metamorphoses* deal with universal laws and processes in an 'imaginative vision of a world where all things are inter-related, where flesh and blood are near kin to soil and river, where man and animal share common instincts'.[22] After he had experienced Ovid, metamorphosis for Dryden (as for Darwin) becomes the universal law that is of most interest to him. By one of those cunning extensions of his author, Dryden sees the law of metamorphosis as including not only history, where 'former Things / Are set aside, like abdicated Kings';[23] but also the specific act of translation itself. To look at it the other way round, what is the metamorphosis of the universe, continually recycling itself, but one unending act of translation too? –

> All Things are alter'd, nothing is destroy'd,
> The shifted Scene, for some new Show employ'd ...
> Those very Elements which we partake,
> Alive, when Dead some other Bodies make:
> Translated grow[24]

Dryden delighted in mirroring his authors one in another – Horace in
Virgil, Virgil in Horace, Spenser in Ovid. Chaucer's Duke Theseus, in
Dryden's version of *The Knight's Tale*, enunciates his philosophy of life
and death, in much the same way as Lucretius. Chaucer's very characters
illustrate types that 'are still remaining in Mankind', Dryden says,
'though they are call'd by other Names than those of *Moncks*, and *Fryars*,
and *Chanons, and Lady Abbesses*',[25] and are part of a universal metamorphosis which is basically indestructible, as resilient as *The Knyghtes
Tale*, now transposed into the acoustic range of the seventeenth-century
reader.

I cannot, alas, deal in detail with Dryden's narrative brilliance in
retelling Ovid's stories, or in retelling stories from Boccaccio and
Chaucer, in *Fables*. After his death, his excerpts from Ovid were to take
their place in the translation of a complete *Metamorphoses*, brought
together by Dr Samuel Garth, the Queen's physician, in 1717. Garth, in
short, reactivated this Dryden–Tonson project, and the result is what I
believe to be the most splendid *Metamorphoses* we have. One third of the
translations in it are by Dryden. Garth drew on the work of several poets
for whom Dryden had set a standard, some of whom are little known
today though they rose to the occasion as translators then – Croxall,
Eusden, Harvey, Maynwaring, Rowe, Stonestreet, Tate, Vernon, and
Garth himself. Congreve is there along with Addison. The most famous
younger presence is Alexander Pope, who at the age of sixteen was
inspired by Dryden to his own metamorphosis of Chaucer, his sparkling
versions of *The Merchant's Tale* and *The Wife of Bath her Prologue*.
Ahead of him lay the *Iliad* and the *Odyssey*, challenged into being by
Dryden's Virgil. Some of the poets in Garth's Ovid were writing in
Dryden's own lifetime, and for all we know Dryden himself may have
revised their versions, since *he* was the editorial presence behind this
book that he was never to see completed and in print.[26] There is a poetic
rightness in the fact that Garth gave the oration at Dryden's funeral. The
success of Garth's Ovid says much about the imaginative climate in the
eighteenth century. That this book (still available in popular editions in
Victorian times, and made so again recently by Wordsworth Classics),
with its powerful erotic charge, should have appeared in the middle of
what used to be called 'our age of prose and reason', dispels somewhat
that misconception of Matthew Arnold's on which many of us were
brought up, and also powerfully illustrates how the idea of metamorphosis
laid hold on the Augustan imagination.

By 1700, then, Dryden had created that part of the idiom and
tradition from which the individual talent could take wing, and he had
done it in large part through translation. Alexander Pope, we all agree,

was the most significant individual talent of the coming era. Paying tribute to Dryden's *Fables Ancient and Modern*, the book that contained his *Metamorphoses* and much else, Pope could say (writing to the old dramatist, William Wycherley),

> those scribblers who attacked [Dryden] in his latter times were only like gnats in a summer evening, which are never very troublesome but in the finest and most glorious season; for his fire, like the sun's, shined clearest towards its setting.[27]

Pope's tribute was to a work mainly of translation, emphasizing what we still choose to forget, namely the centrality of poetic translation to the whole history of English poetry. That history has to be rewritten, because the presence of translation in it changes the balance of conventional assessment that still often rates poetic translation as a poor cousin of original verse. For too long, Dryden was looked on merely as a satirist and controversialist (which he magnificently was), but the fire of which Pope speaks that 'shin'd most clearly towards its setting' was that of a great poet, the measure of whose greatness can only be taken if we see him as a great translator too.

NOTES

1. *Lives*, I, 410.
2. Congreve's remark is found in the Epistle Dedicatory to Tonson's edition of Dryden's dramatic works, and is quoted here from *Dryden: The Critical Heritage*, edited by James and Helen Kinsley (London, 1971), p. 264.
3. Donald Carne-Ross, 'A Mistaken Ambition of Exactness', *Delos*, 2 (1968), 171–95.
4. *Aurelian Townshend's Poems and Masks*, edited by E. K. Chambers (Oxford, 1912), p. 43.
5. *The Poetical Works of Sir John Denham*, edited by Theodore Howard Banks, second edition (Hamden, CT, 1969), pp. 159–60.
6. 'To Sir *Richard Fanshaw* upon his Translation of *Pastor Fido*', 16–17, 21–4; *Works of Denham*, pp. 143–4.
7. 'On Mr. Abraham Cowley his Death and Burial Amongst the Ancient Poets', 35–8; *Works of Denham*, p. 150.
8. Donald Davie, *Purity of Diction in English Verse* (London, 1952), p. 65.
9. Ezra Pound, *ABC of Reading* (London, 1961), p. 113.
10. *The English Writings of Abraham Cowley*, edited by A. R. Waller, 2 vols (Cambridge, 1905; hereafter 'Cowley'), II, 457. The following prose quotations are taken from the same page.
11. Preface to *Pindarique Odes* (1668); Cowley, I, 156.
12. *Virgil: The Georgics, with John Dryden's Translation*, edited by Alistair Elliot (Ashington, 1981), p. 11.

13. D. S. Carne-Ross, 'Jocasta's Divine Head: English with a Foreign Accent', *Arion*, third series 1.i (1990), 106–42 (pp. 106–7).

14. Eric Griffiths, 'Dryden's Past', *PBA*, 84 (1994), 113–49 (p. 127).

15. *An Essay on Translated Verse*, 95–100; quoted from *Augustan Critical Writing*, edited by David Womersley (Harmondsworth, 1997), p. 111.

16. Lines 179–82; *Augustan Critical Writing*, p. 113.

17. Dedication to *The Spanish Friar*; *Works*, XIV, 100.

18. MS note by Jonathan Richardson Senior on p. cxix of his annotated copy of *Remarks on Milton's Paradise Lost by Jonathan Richardson Father and Son* (1734), now in the London Library.

19. 'Paraphrase upon Horace. Book I. Ode XXXI', 1–6; quoted from *The Poems of John Oldham*, edited by Harold F. Brooks (Oxford, 1987), p. 118.

20. Paul Hammond, *John Oldham and the Renewal of Classical Culture* (Cambridge, 1983), p. 3. The following quotation is from p. 133.

21. Preface to *Sylvae*; *Poems*, II, 249.

22. I quote from my own *Poetry and Metamorphosis* (Cambridge, 1983), p. 2.

23. *Of the Pythagorean Philosophy*, 274–5; Kinsley, IV, 1725.

24. *Of the Pythagorean Philosophy*, 388–9, 394–6; Kinsley, IV, 1727–8.

25. Preface to *Fables*; Kinsley, IV, 1455.

26. For Dryden's role among contributors to the composite volume see David Hopkins, 'Dryden and the Garth-Tonson Ovid', *RES*, 39 (1988), 64–74, and addendum, *RES*, 51 (2000), 83–9.

27. *The Works of Pope*, edited by Whitwell Elwin and William John Courthope, Vol. VI: *Correspondence, I* (London, 1871), p. 16.

Dryden: Poet or Translator?

Felicity Rosslyn

The tercentenary of Dryden's death finds his reputation secure. The ongoing Longman and the nearly complete California editions give Dryden as much space on the library shelves as Pope, and almost as much as Milton. Whether he *was* a poet, and whether what he wrote was poetry – two questions the nineteenth century debated at length – seem issues as dead as the terms they were couched in. Even the distinctions his strongest admirers always made, that his versification was often careless and its emotional content specious (as Johnson put it, 'he could more easily fill the ear with some splendid novelty than awaken those ideas that slumber in the heart', *Lives*, I, 459), are reservations that seem to have lost their point.

But a long controversy is rarely unprovoked, though the terms in which it was played out may be in need of vigorous redefinition, and in this essay I want to suggest other ways of understanding why Dryden's status as a poet has been controversial in the past, and might still be felt to be difficult. Critical consensus can always be a cover for inertia, we know, and even admirers may be glad of an opportunity to reassess the grounds of their enthusiasm. In this spirit, one important question that could be raised is: *which* Dryden is it who is still 'alive'? That is, does anyone read the works of Dryden without selecting heavily and leaving aside large areas of his achievement?

One way of responding to this fact is not to interpret it at all; Dryden simply wrote a great deal in different genres and no-one is going to be equal to the whole corpus. 'Here is God's plenty', we might say, as he so cheerfully does of Chaucer's works (Preface to *Fables*, Kinsley, IV, 1455). But there seems to be more to interpret than this, even by Dryden's own account. His working career is disjunctive, studded with regretful afterthoughts and self-accusations. His repudiation of his plays, in particular, could not be more strongly stated than in *To Mrs. Anne Killigrew*:

> O wretched we, why were we hurried down
>   This lubric and adulterate age
> (Nay added fat pollutions of our own)
> T' increase the steaming ordures of the stage?
>   (62–5; *Poems*, III, 10)

And in the *Fables* he takes care to stress the implicit morality of all his stories because 'I wish I could affirm with a safe Conscience, that I had taken the same Care in all my former Writings' (Preface; Kinsley, IV, 1447). On the front of public morality, Dryden did feel he had apologies to make, and we might agree that the obscurity into which most of the plays have fallen is not undeserved. *The Kind Keeper* is a farrago of bawdy cant such as only a lexicographer could find interesting. (The author of the much more obscene *Sodom*, probably Rochester, is at least involved in, and excited by, his linguistic offensiveness – Dryden is only remorselessly lewd.) When Dryden rewrites *Oedipus*, there is no doubt of the incestuous passion between Oedipus and Jocasta: they comment on it in pseudo-innocent detail. And Dryden's adaptations of Shakespeare are startlingly coarse. This is what he makes of Prospero's anxious love for Miranda in the *Tempest*, when Dryden's character warns his daughter against 'wild young men':

> *Prosp.* ... they are wild within Doors, in Chambers,
> And in Closets.
> *Dor.* But Father, I would stroak 'em and make 'em gentle,
> Then sure they would not hurt me.
> *Prosp.* You must not trust them, Child: no woman can come
> Neer 'em but she feels a pain full nine Months.
> (II.iv; *Works*, X, 40–1)

Since Dryden collaborated with Davenant in this play he may not be responsible for these particular lines, but the whole version is a tissue of leers and winks, and he must be the author of some of them.

There is a school of thought that says when a handsome apology is made it should be accepted and the occasion forgotten. Dryden's apology in *To Mrs. Anne Killigrew* is heartfelt, but we may still wonder why, if Dryden could deplore his own works so much in retrospect, he was capable of writing them at all. Harsh interpretations have been put on this fact: Cowper, reading Johnson's 'Life of Dryden' in 1784, comments: 'What a sycophant to the public taste was Dryden, sinning against his feelings, lewd in his writings, though chaste in his conversation.' It might be thought that Cowper would naturally be unsympathetic to Dryden, but in fact he thought 'his faults are those of a great man', and he much preferred him to Pope, on the same grounds as Johnson.[1] What struck him as notable was rather that Dryden's feelings were not of a piece with his writing: that he seemed detached from his own lewdness, and in a sense, Dryden did not *mean* what he wrote. Cowper calls this being 'a sycophant to the public taste'; and without using moralistic terms, we may still wonder how

Dryden picked up the low norms and expectations of the audience for which he wrote, and managed to supply them so accurately. Did he lack an internal monitor to tell him when he was writing something he would later regret? Would he have understood what Cowper means by that phrase 'sinning against his feelings' – or did he simply wake up from time to time, like a sleepwalker, and realize what he had been doing with his art?

This question about Dryden's internal monitor can be posed in terms of the political poems also. In any collection of the complete poems, the *Heroic Stanzas* ('Consecrated to the Glorious Memory Of his most Serene and Renowned Highness Oliver, Late Lord Protector of this Commonwealth') lie cheek-by-jowl with *Astraea Redux* ('A Poem on the Happy Restoration and Return of His Sacred Majesty Charles the Second'). Like almost everyone else in England, Dryden made a rapid and successful adjustment of his loyalties in 1660; he had walked in Cromwell's funeral cortege, along with Marvell and Milton, but he found no difficulty in welcoming the restoration of the monarchy.

We have grown out of labelling poets 'turncoats' for this kind of behaviour; we understand all too well how social and economic pressures operate on societies in rapid transition, and we can see how a poet who prized order as highly as Dryden might find it in Cromwell at one time, and in the monarchy at another. The real issue lies elsewhere – in whether Dryden meant what he said about either Cromwell or Charles, and how far he followed through their implications in his own mind. A Lord Protector and a King represent two kinds of royalty that no-one can really embrace simultaneously. Dryden praises Cromwell's *natural* authority without seeming to feel that after acknowledging that a man may become king by inner force, he cannot then praise Charles's *divine* and *inherited* authority. Cromwell, victor in Scotland and Ireland, is a kind of star, or a golden lodestone:

18
Nor was he like those stars which only shine
When to pale mariners they storms portend;
He had his calmer influence, and his mine
Did love and majesty together blend.

19
'Tis true, his count'nance did imprint an awe,
And naturally all souls to his did bow;
As wands of divination downward draw
And point to beds where sovereign gold doth grow.
                    (*Heroic Stanzas*, 69–76; *Poems*, I, 23–4)

Cromwell, says Dryden, was a king in every sense that matters, a regal compound of love and majesty, and men's souls registered his sovereignty like so many metal detectors.

But in Charles, without any sense of incongruity, Dryden alleges that England finds a Christ-like pardoner for its sins, a king descended from both heavenly and earthly lineage. The very cliffs of Dover reach out to him for absolution:

> And welcome now, great monarch, to your own;
> Behold th' approaching cliffs of Albion ...
> The land returns, and in the white it wears
> The marks of penitence and sorrow bears.
> But you, whose goodness your descent doth show,
> Your heavenly parentage, and earthly too;
> By that same mildness which your father's crown
> Before did ravish, shall secure your own.
> (*Astraea Redux*, 250–1, 254–9; *Poems*, I, 50)

Obviously, Dryden was a public poet, and this is the kind of thing that public poets do; they cry 'le roi est mort, vive le roi!', and so too, we might think, would we if we had lived at the time.

But for most poets this central and most agonizingly divisive issue of the seventeenth century, the question of what gives a king the right to rule, is argued out deep inside them. The Restoration leaves them with an almost intolerable internal conflict which manifests itself in furious forms of energy. *Paradise Lost* is among the after-shocks; but *Astraea Redux* is certainly not. It is possible to say that this is because Dryden was too wise to get involved, and that he was never an ideologue, which is an excellent thing, but the net effect is that there is a lot of Dryden's poetry that he seems not to have 'meant' in the way that other people mean things. Perhaps this is why we select so vigorously when we read Dryden, and do not feel that we are doing anything odd; because what we are neglecting is so obviously not really what Dryden 'meant'.

Another interesting problem, to which readers in the past were much more sensitive than ourselves, is Dryden's conversion to Catholicism in 1685. The fact that it was sincere enough to last a lifetime has put it beyond polite discussion. If, however, we ask not about Dryden's apparent opportunism, but about the implications of Catholicism if he embraced it sincerely, we come up with a quite different concern. What did it mean for someone raised in a vigorously Puritan family that he submitted to the authority of the Pope, assented to the miracle of transubstantiation, and agreed to view the evolution of rationalism as a disastrous error?

To see it in terms of intellectual history, joining the Catholic church meant a tremendous division of his mental life. If the keynote of modernity is that it lays all thoughts side by side and tries to make them cohere, allowing no special sanctity or prestige to one idea over another, then Catholicism is a deliberate bulwark against modernity.[2] It replaces enquiry with authority, and reason with mystery, *tout court*; and one way of understanding why the religious struggles of the seventeenth century were so bitterly factional is that the modern mind was evolving so rapidly and reacting so angrily against each of its previous incarnations. Anglicans repudiated Catholicism (no miracles!), Puritans repudiated Anglicans (no rituals!), and Quakers repudiated Puritans (no forms at all!), as each allowed ever less validity to external authority, and took responsibility for the coherence and truth of their beliefs on an ever more personal footing (losing sight of God, a Catholic would say, ever more completely in the process).[3]

Everything about Dryden before his conversion declares him to be a member of this secular, modern society created by the brutal demystification of the monarchy in 1649 and completed by the Restoration of the Stuarts in the disenchanting form of Charles II. In 1681 he is equally funny about English disorder and about the Catholic solution: the English are

> God's pampered people, whom, debauched with ease,
> No king could govern, nor no god could please
> (Gods they had tried of every shape and size
> That god-smiths could produce, or priests devise)
> (*Absalom and Achitophel*, 47–50; *Poems*, I, 458–9)

And the Catholic French (the 'Jebusites') are a political fifth column who swallow the absurdity of transubstantiation:

> Th' Egyptian rites the Jebusites embraced,
> Where gods were recommended by their taste:
> Such savoury deities must needs be good
> Who serve at once for worship and for food.
> By force they could not introduce these gods,
> For ten to one in former days was odds,
> So fraud was used
> (118–24; *Poems*, I, 464)

If by 1685 he was assenting to the miraculous transubstantiation of the wafer himself, does this mean that he had forgotten these jokes, or repented of them, or that he never meant them in the first place? We cannot know, but we do know that he made a decision to put a stop to the journey these jokes imply (the journey Rochester, for instance, made). Dryden drew a line under intellectual modernity on his own account.

Creating a large area of his mental life where reason had to give way to mystery, and a sense of comedy was subdued to the sacred, was bound to have consequences for his writing. One way of saying what makes *The Hind and the Panther* (1687) so painful to read is that it evinces so little of Dryden's real mental power, and yet is so laden with argument. It has the vices of fancy, and of reason as well. The animal fable, so shrewdly parodied by Prior, is several centuries too late for serious application; and it skews the argument in advance by declaring the Catholic and Anglican churches to be quite different animals (one pure Hind, one spotted Panther) – when the real problem is that they are varieties of the same animal. It has the vices of excessive rationality too: Dryden's argument boils down to the fact that if he can believe in the Incarnation and the Trinity, he cannot sensibly object to transubstantiation (ll. 79–135) – a kind of intellectual evolution in reverse. And he commits himself to a life based purely on faith in language so rational as to verge on parody:

> Rest then, my soul, from endless anguish freed,
> Nor sciences thy guide, nor sense thy creed.
> Faith is the best ensurer of thy bliss:
> The bank above must fail before the venture miss.
>   (I, 146–9; *Poems*, III, 60)

Pascal thought he might 'wager' on Christianity, but to bank on it as 'insurance' is surely the wrong metaphor. What does convince in this poem, however, is Dryden's determination to withdraw from the struggle, his need to free his soul from 'endless anguish' because earthly guides have proved inadequate to his spiritual security. Perhaps, to return to our earlier formulation, he recognized that he did not have an 'internal monitor', and so he welcomed the firmest kind of external one.

This may have worked for Dryden as a person (he sent his children to Rome, and one son even became a priest), but the issue for literary criticism is whether his poetry after 1685 shows the consequences. And certainly there is something new going on in his writing which might be viewed as the other side of the coin, one side of which is the thin apologetics of *The Hind and the Panther*: the joyful assertion of a pagan reality in which there are no miracles whatever, and no life after death.

Nature rules supreme, and man's sole obligation is to live fully in the present – because the time will come when he feels nothing, one way or the other. At the same time Dryden was joining the Catholic church he was translating Lucretius 'Against the Fear of Death':

> The worst that can befall thee, measured right,
> Is a sound slumber, and a long good night.
> Yet thus the fools, that would be thought the wits,
> Disturb their mirth with melancholy fits,
> When healths go round, and kindly brimmers flow,
> Till the fresh garlands on their foreheads glow,
> They whine, and cry, 'Let us make haste to live,
> Short are the joys that human life can give'.
> Eternal preachers, that corrupt the draught,
> And pall the god that never thinks with thought;
> Idiots with all that thought, to whom the worst
> Of death is want of drink, and endless thirst,
> Or any fond desire as vain as these.
> For ev'n in sleep, the body wrapped in ease
> Supinely lies, as in the peaceful grave,
> And wanting nothing, nothing can it crave.
>
> (95–110; *Poems*, II, 321)

The bounding rhythms, the verbal energy, and the genial scorn of this are all characteristic of Dryden's writing after his conversion. We may wonder whether, in some paradoxical way, they may also be the consequences of it. What kind of energy is he releasing, and what exactly are the components of this free-flowing scorn?

It is a familiar paradox in Dryden criticism that for an author so supportive of order he is deeply drawn to disorder, and Johnson commented long ago on the irrational brinkmanship of his art. Dryden's favourite mode, says Johnson, was argument, and –

> Next to argument, his delight was in wild and daring sallies of sentiment, in the irregular and excentrick violence of wit. He delighted to tread upon the brink of meaning, where light and darkness begin to mingle; to approach the precipice of absurdity, and hover over the abyss of unideal vacancy.
>
> (*Lives*, I, 460)

One way of understanding this compulsion in Dryden is as a kind of spiritual vertigo, the same vertigo that draws him to Lucretius at the very moment of his conversion. He is fascinated by what lies over the brink of meaning. He has no intention of falling over, of running the risk that Rochester did and finding that his real subject lies over the chasm ('Upon Nothing'). But in the voice of a pagan he can say everything he denies *in propria persona*, and with an overplus of defiance and scorn that are perhaps directed at himself as much as anyone.

The formidable power of the Lucretius translation raises another question: does it matter that, as David Hopkins phrases it, 'the vast bulk of his work after 1687 (and almost all the best) was to be devoted to the results of his spiritual communings with a number of congenial master-spirits from pagan Greece and Rome'[4] – or, as less sympathetic critics have seen it, that Dryden dwindled from a poet to a translator? This is another area where we view things differently from the past: much neo-classic criticism of the last thirty years has been devoted to dispelling the assumption that translation is a secondary activity. We accept more fully than we did that great translations are the work of great poets, and much of Dryden's current standing derives from this fact. But there may be a kernel of truth in the old suspicion that clung to translation – which is that no translator starts where the original poet started, with the need to generate his own myth or story. The translator finds the subject and its form already supplied; his inner world is never as fully exposed to the reader as his author's is. His translation may hint and imply many things, but he does not carry the same responsibility for its existence that the author does.

Is it possible that the division of Dryden's mental life by Catholicism meant that he could not, or did not dare, generate large structures of meaning from inside himself? Did he suspect that he lacked the internal coherence? Some such explanation seems to be required for the remarkable fact that aside from his prose, and a few odes and epistles, Dryden never speaks in his own voice again. At the stage in his career when a great poet usually exerts his utmost powers to bring his sense of the relation of the visible world to the invisible into public form – the stage at which Milton wrote *Paradise Lost* and Pope *An Essay on Man* – Dryden translated the *Æneid*. And whatever the obvious virtues of his translation, no-one has ever mistaken it for a *profession de foi*. Dryden himself thought Homer 'more according to my Genius, than the *Latin* Poet' (Preface to *Fables*; Kinsley, IV, 1448), and he got as much, if not more pleasure out of translating Juvenal.

A 'great poet', if the phrase means more than a personal preference, would be the writer who writes simultaneously on his own behalf and on behalf of his age, who is read with excitement and gratitude because he solves emotional and intellectual problems that are pressing in some form on all his readers. In this sense, the greatness of *Paradise Lost* would be that it confronts the seventeenth-century conundrum, 'What is the relation of authority to free will?', dramatizes the feelings involved, and offers a solution. (Whether it satisfies us now, of course, is another issue.) *An Essay on Man* confronts the eighteenth-century development of this problem, in a world in which God has more or less retired from view: 'What are the uses of reason, and its limits?' The urgency of this question and the vitality of Pope's answer are more or less lost to us now, but the evidence of the usefulness of what he wrote is the way it swept across Europe – because in solving the question for his own culture, Pope solved it for many others.

Although there could be other explanations of why Dryden did not write his equivalent great work, beginning with his loss of the Laureateship, the fact that it is missing necessarily makes a difference to our sense of what kind of poet he was. It may be worth noting, too, that we have external ratification of the problem of his status from a European perspective: although he is a great translator, he is not translated; other continental cultures do not seem to have felt much need of him.[5] We might hazard the guess that what he represents is what continental Europe already had in abundance: the spirit of the Counter-Reformation, the decision to put stability before free enquiry.

One objection that could be made to the drift of these remarks would be that Dryden's translations do amount to a world-view, if properly understood – that they can be decoded as a profound response to seventeenth-century questions in themselves. Can we read them, however masked, as Dryden's original statement? Some attractive criticism has been written on this assumption; and indeed the Juvenal satires, the Horace odes, and the Chaucer versions do each give a strong sense of a coherent world-view, and of Dryden's self-discovery in his author. There is a problem, however, with this very success: it seems extraordinary that someone who relishes Juvenal's lack of proportion as Dryden so deeply does, can enter with equal conviction into Horace's fine poise, or Chaucer's Christian humanism. What kind of writer could find room in his imagination for Persius, in addition – and not Virgil *or* Homer, but Virgil *and* Homer? Since Dryden obviously does, what freedom does he have that most of us do not?

The puzzle is that Dryden's sympathetic insights do not seem to commit him beyond the limits of each poem. For instance, Sigismonda's famous self-defence in *Sigismonda and Guiscardo* would seem to represent a wonderful maturation of Dryden's otherwise rather crude approach to female psychology. Here, via Boccaccio (but considerably altered), is what the mature Dryden can do on a subject which formerly only elicited the Restoration note, the subject of women and sexual appetite. In this passage Sigismonda reproaches Tancred for not giving her a second husband:

> Thy little Care to mend my Widow'd Nights }
> Has forc'd me to recourse of Marriage-Rites, }
> To fill an empty Side, and follow known Delights. }
> What have I done in this, deserving Blame?
> State-Laws may alter: Nature's are the same;
> Those are usurp'd on helpless Woman-kind,
> Made without our Consent, and wanting Pow'r to bind.
>   Thou, *Tancred*, better should'st have understood,
> That as thy Father gave thee Flesh and Blood,
> So gav'st thou me
>   (414–24; Kinsley, IV, 1556)

This is surely the heroic note: Sigismonda says 'I am what I am' and affirms that men and women are made of the same materials. She has made her choice, and she takes the fatal consequences nobly. A good case could be made for saying that Dryden's attitude here has evolved through his translation of Juvenal's Sixth Satire and Dido's speeches in *Æneid* IV; that translation for Dryden is a method of research and discovery.

But when we read on through the *Fables* and see what else he was writing at the same time, it is harder to be sure. In one of the few poems in which he does use his own voice, 'To My Honor'd Kinsman, John Driden', he falls into a stale mode of bachelor wit, and congratulates his kinsman on never having married in sub-Miltonic terms:

> Lord of your self, uncumber'd with a Wife;
> Where, for a Year, a Month, perhaps a Night,
> Long penitence succeeds a short Delight:
> Minds are so hardly match'd, that ev'n the first,
> Though pair'd by Heav'n, in Paradise, were curs'd.
> For Man and Woman, though in one they grow,
> Yet, first or last, return again to Two.
> He to God's Image, she to His was made;
> So, farther from the Fount, the stream at random stray'd ...
>   Not that my Verse would blemish all the Fair; }
> But yet if *some* be bad, 'tis Wisdom to beware; }
> And better shun the Bait, than struggle in the Snare. }
>   (18–26, 31–3; Kinsley, IV, 1530)

It is hard to deny that this is at least as characteristic of Dryden as Sigismonda's noble speech – including his half-retraction, 'Not that my verse would blemish all the fair'. In the same way, Dryden prints his joyfully offensive translation of Juvenal's Satire VI on women with the bland assurance, 'Whatever his Roman ladies were, the English are free from all his imputations' ('Argument'; *Poems*, IV, 45–6). He invites us to say that he does not 'mean' what he writes, but we are left with the puzzle of what then drove him to write it.

There is a memorable formulation by Coleridge which may relate to this puzzle: 'Dryden's genius was of that sort which catches fire by its own motion; his chariot wheels get hot by driving fast.'[6] Dryden can find a subject in almost any direction, and as he pursues it, his language glows with kinetic energy. By the same token, he 'finds' himself in a wide variety of disparate and mutually contradictory authors, and for as long as he writes – and only so long – he shares his author's world-view. We are free to say either that we rejoice in his scope and diversity, or that we are disconcerted not to find very much of him anywhere. What is certain is that we will enjoy the vigor of his language; but we may also wonder if its superabundant energy is not the by-product of Dryden's equivocal commitment to what he is saying.

Perhaps the clearest way of framing the question of Dryden's poetical achievement is to focus on a few lines that have attracted universal praise, in which Dryden seems to sum up the whole problem of his age. This is the famous chorus from the *Secular Masque*:

> *All, all, of a piece throughout;*
> *Thy Chase had a Beast in View; [to Diana]*
> *Thy Wars brought nothing about; [to Mars]*
> *Thy Lovers were all untrue. [to Venus]*
> *'Tis well an Old Age is out,*
> *And time to begin a New.*
> (92–7; Kinsley, IV, 1765)

This masque ends with a 'dance of Huntsmen, Nymphs, Warriours and Lovers', because there is no plot and there is really nothing else to say; and the verbal energy and rhythmic power of these lines should not blind us to the fact that they are an expression of despair, however genially admitted. Do Dryden's last words signal his awareness that he has been as deeply involved in the errors of his age as anyone?

NOTES

1. Quoted from *Dryden: The Critical Heritage*, edited by James and Helen Kinsley (London, 1971), pp. 313–14.

2. As Ernest Gellner usefully puts it, 'the secret of the modern spirit' is that 'all facts are located within a continuous logical space ... so that in principle one single language describes the world and is internally unitary' – as opposed to 'pre-rational' visions which allow the co-existence of 'hierarchically related sub-worlds, and the existence of special privileged facts, sacralized and exempt from ordinary treatment' (*Nations and Nationalism* (Oxford, 1983), p. 21).

3. Anyone who considers these to be religious issues rather than intellectual ones might try to enter into the present Pope's mental world for a moment. He holds that he was saved from assassination in 1981 by the miraculous intervention of Our Lady of Fatima. He has placed the near-fatal bullet in the crown of her statue in Portugal.

4. David Hopkins, *John Dryden* (Cambridge, 1986), p. 131.

5. A few of the plays travelled to France in the eighteenth century, and he is much valued in Germany as a thesis subject, but he has not been incorporated in the same way as, say, Pope (*The Essay on Criticism* and *The Rape of the Lock* were quickly translated, as well as *An Essay on Man*).

6. *Coleridge's Miscellaneous Criticism*, edited by Thomas Middleton Raysor (London, 1936), p. 431.

Teaching Troubling Texts: Virgil, Dryden, and Exemplary Translation

Jan Parker

> Poor hapless Youth! what Praises can be paid
> To Love so great, to such transcendent Store
> Of early Worth, and sure Presage of more?
> Accept what e're *Æneas* can afford ...
> Thy Body on thy Parents I bestow, ⎫
> To rest thy Soul, at least if Shadows know, ⎬
> Or have a sense of human Things below. ⎭
> There to thy fellow Ghosts with Glory tell,
> 'Twas by the great *Æneas* hand I fell.
> (1169–72, 1176–80; Works, VI, 714)

When Dryden translated Æneas' address to Lausus, he cut out Æneas' epithet, *pius*, and made less pointed the direct question of the original:

> Quid tibi nunc, miserande puer, pro laudibus istis?
> Quid pius Æneas tanta dabit indole dignum?[1]

> (What will *pius* Æneas now give to match such merit ... ?)

– turning it into an elegiac rhetorical question: 'what Praises can be paid ...?' Does it matter? I think it does; that the move from direct to rhetorical question is symptomatic of a suppression of what I argue below to be a troubled and troubling voice in the *Æneid*: the voice of Æneas. Any such omissions are to be noted not as faults: no reader of Dryden, of all poets, should resort to such a simplistic judgement. Rather, a great poet-translator's suppressions or expansions are to be attended to as the result of his close, personal, emulative engagement with the text. Indeed, I argue in what follows that they should be attended to by all those reading and teaching classic texts: that the places where the translator's work reveals knots, difficulties, and what is for his time and readership 'untranslatable', are just as important as those places where the text is brought alive by the finest of poetic re-imagining.

Chapman spoke for many later translators when he described his aim in translating Homer into English as being 'with Poesie to open Poesie'.[2] This paper argues that such poetic re-creations of classic texts should not just be appreciated as independent creations, but should be harnessed with annotated literal translations to the study of the original text. Classical texts cannot today be read as if they were written today; nor can modern readers, whatever their linguistic ability, read them as their original readers did. All have to 'translate': to enter into an imaginative dialogue with a densely and complexly allusive text across time, culture, and language. Classic translations provide, at least, previous contributions to the dialogue.

More, they provide *exempla* of works that are themselves exemplary, works which are concerned with interpreting and evaluating 'heroic' characters and significant actions. Classic translations serve as *exempla* – as both shining achievement and challenge to later readers and translators. Dryden's Virgil and Pope's Homer are also translations of classics – works accorded the status of a benchmark of literary achievement for their own and later cultures, and which demand readings appreciative of literary and cultural depth and complexity. Classical works, like the Greek texts for the Romans who were 'captivated' by them,[3] serve as emulative challenges – as achievements that a poet-translator has to live up to, to measure himself and be measured against. They challenge, also, the modern reader: in demanding that the reader respond to and evaluate 'heroic' characters and actions, they require complex self-positioning and the skill of reading an alien yet engaging and implicating text.

The characters whose actions form the material of classical epic and tragedy are uneasily situated against the society within the text. As 'heroes' of stature and mythic background, their actions and fate are set against a normative framework which may challenge that of an internal or external audience. Epic and tragedy reflect as well as reflecting on the problematic position of the hero in society – presenting the heroic question as multi-faceted, ambiguous, or multivalent. Readers and translators have to come to an understanding of the values the hero lives by or questions, of whether he embodies or transgresses the norms of his society; in short, in what respect his psychology and actions are presented as exemplary. The translator must then decide how to render them for his own society. Dryden writes in 1693:

> what poems have not, with time, received an alteration in their fashion? Which alteration, says Holyday, is to aftertimes as good a

warrant as the first. Has not Virgil changed the manners of Homer's heroes in his *Aeneis*? Certainly he has, and for the better. For Virgil's age was more civilized, and better bred.[4]

Virgil's changes are those of a translator, charged with bringing Homer's exemplary text into Augustan culture. In his *Æneis*, Dryden's sensibility as a translator is matched against a poetic and heroic sensibility in the text: with a poet, and a hero, who are both all too conscious of their exemplary status. Both Virgil's text and Dryden's translation serve as witness that *exempla* can inspire but also burden those who have to live up to them.

Virgil's Æneas is a character conscious of a past classical model. In Book XII, following reference after reference to the recuperation of Troy's past, there is a rare direct dialogue between Æneas and someone he loves, a rare insight into his relationship with past and present. Armed for the single combat that will finish the epic and his struggle to win a place for his son's future empire in Italy, Æneas addresses his son for the first and only time. Æneas 'folded his son Ascanius in a mailed embrace', Virgil says, 'and lightly kissing his lips through the helmet's open visor, he said':

> Disce, puer, virtutem ex me, verumque laborem;
> Fortunam ex aliis.

(Learn fortitude and toil from me, my son, ache of true toil. Good fortune learn from others.)

> Sis memor: & te animo repetentem exempla tuorum,
> Et pater Æneas, & avunculus excitet Hector.

(Do not forget, but rather, dwelling upon your kinsmen's example, remember and be stirred by your father Æneas and your uncle Hector.)[5]

Æneas' presentation of himself and Hector as *exempla* is shot through with difficulty. His actions throughout the *Æneid* have not always been exemplary, to say the least; and the simple allusion to himself and his uncle Hector as univocal *exempla* is complicated by the complex allusion to the Iliadic Hector. There is also in his words an allusion to Sophocles' Ajax saying farewell to *his* young son before committing suicide:

> My boy, have better luck [*eutuchesteros*] than your father had, be like him in all else and you will not be base.
>
> (*Ajax* 550–1)

Accius' Latin version of Sophocles has Ajax say: 'be equal in *virtus*, unequal in *fortuna* to your father' (*Trag.* fr. 156).[6] This whole scene of the father bidding farewell to his son before going out to war is itself uneasily positioned as an *exemplum*, its status complicated by allusive references and proleptic foreshadowing – verbal allusion to Ajax in Sophocles and Accius bidding farewell to Eurysaces, visual allusion to Hector's farewell to Astyanax. The effect of the first is to throw forward a shadow over Æneas' climactic defeat of Turnus, since this scene, in which Æneas is in fact going out not to die but to kill Turnus, is overcast by associations with the madness and self-destruction of Ajax.

The overlay of this scene on that in the *Iliad* of Hector's farewell, as so often where Æneas is bound to replay the past, shows an Æneas who is inhibited. Both fathers are armed; both sons are affected by it. Ascanius is distanced from Æneas' embrace – he receives 'an armed embrace' and is 'kissed through the helmet'. Astyanax is not. The baby is frightened by the horsehair crest on his father's helmet, and cries. Andromache laughs through her tears, and Hector, taking his helmet off, kisses his infant son and tosses him in his arms (*Iliad*, VI, 471–4).

The comparison is informative: Æneas stays behind the helmet that keeps his son away, Hector takes it off; Æneas enfolds Ascanius in a mailed embrace, Hector takes his son in his arms. Hector, following heroic *exempla*, goes out, as he must, to fight and die; Æneas going out, as *he* must, to protect Ascanius' and Rome's future importance, is inhibited from acting naturally here, as in Troy in Book II, and as in Carthage. Whatever the effect of the allusion here – perhaps pointing up the barrier that Rome's fate places between Æneas and those he loves (remember *pius* Æneas, who longed to soothe Dido but left wordlessly, obedient to the gods in *Æneid* IV, 384ff.) – it shows *pius* Æneas is bound up with the Homeric past and Augustan future, as Virgil himself was. The *Æneid* shows an Æneas himself caught between *exempla* – the heroes of the Trojan War whose defeat he is to avenge, and the line of images of the Augustan future, seen in the underworld in procession like those busts carried by the young members of the Roman family at Roman funerals to ensure and exhort imitation. Virgil was of course likewise so bound – to imitate and transcend Homer while transforming the classic text into a Roman and Augustan one.

Modern students come to the *Æneid* with little of the linguistic and cultural grounding they need to read and locate classic texts. They need to translate the complex cultural self-positioning of the hero, the various and perhaps conflicting voices and narratorial judgements of the text – a difficult process of translation that goes beyond the superficial language transaction commonly taken as 'translating' a Latin text. Few students have sufficient linguistic sensitivity to perform such translation for themselves, but all students can be shown how to use the classic translators' engagement to break open the texts. This is possible because the classic translator likewise has to come to terms with the text's status as *exemplum*, to 'translate' the double location in past and present, the simultaneous alienness yet visceral oneness that classic texts somehow effect. The translator's double responsibility to both his source-text and source-culture on the one hand, and to his audience in his own culture on the other, shows continuously – not so much in the notes and introduction as in the actual translating decisions made. This double focus puts him into the same unstable position as Æneas – doubly bound, yet reflecting on and enacting the double bind.

A classic translation performs a double function. On the one hand it provides an example of engagement, of poetic communication and embodiment across cultures and languages. On the other, it is an instance of the difficulties and dangers of such embodiment: of suppressions of troubling voices in the text, of cultural appropriation in order to provide its audience with such words as, in Dryden's formulation, 'if [the poet] were living, and an Englishman … he would probably have written' (Preface to *Sylvae*; *Poems*, II, 238).

The difficulty of reading a classic text lies in its challenges and its very alienness: its distance in time and culture, its complex relationship with other contemporary and past texts. The difficulty of teaching a classic text is to find ways of enabling students to engage with complexly situated, distanced, 'classic' texts. Classic translations such as Dryden's serve as preeminent examples of both the challenge and the complex results of such an engagement. But in order to engage in this way, students have to come to terms with translation as an activity, a process as well as a product. They must engage themselves in the bridging of cultures as well as language that is involved in the translation of a classic text. They have to find ways of opening the text for themselves, getting through the voices of the translation to the voices in the original text. In order to enable them to work on the text in this way the teacher has to lay beside the 'classic' translation a bald, under-interpreted text, one which signals that the work of producing a reading is still to be done. That is to say that there is also a place next to the great poet-translator's version for that of, in Denham's words, a 'servile' translator: a 'literal' or crib from someone 'tracing word by word and line by line'. Denham's strictures –

> Nor ought a Genius lesse than his that writ,
> Attempt Translation ...
> That servile path thou nobly dost decline

> Of tracing word by word, and line by line ...
> They but preserve the Ashes, thou the Flame,
> True to his sense, but truer to his fame.[7]

– are appropriate to a reading public that can judge the translation against the classic text, can read the translation intertextually, hearing the Latin behind. It stresses translation of classic texts as an emulative activity. Bearing in mind the very different skills of today's readers, I want to suggest the possibility of using classic translations next to literal, pedestrian versions in order to open other readings: to start a dialogue between creative and literal representations of the source-text. Comparing translations can lead to a more reflective reading of the original; it can also lead to a more appropriately multi-voiced, multi-layered reading. For reading classic texts is in itself a process of translation – of moving towards and relating to texts from a different culture which are themselves consciously and problematically in relationship with the past.

My teaching texts come in threes: a heavily annotated literal translation laid next to the original text, set against a classic translation. The notes – references to echoes of earlier texts and other uses of the key words – turn the 'crib' into a 'glossed text' similar to medieval texts which carried vernacular translations and marginal notes to biblical parallels, types/ antitypes, and scholia. In the example above, Æneas' words to Ascanius, it points up the use of key words (*virtus*, *pius/pietas*, *fortuna*, *exemplum*), the Sophoclean echo and its Latinization in Accius, and details of the Iliadic parallel. Next to this text is laid the Dryden translation: a conjunction that immediately points to the loss when poetry is translated by anyone but a 'Genius'. It also, perhaps, suggests that Dryden's version carries none of the overlay of tragedy and prolepsis (a late twentieth-century concern?) of the glossed text:

> Learn *virtus* and toil from me, my son, ache of true toil.
> *Fortuna* learn from others ...
> Do not forget, but rather, dwelling upon your kinsmen's *exempla*,
> remember and be stirred by your father Æneas and your uncle
> Hector.
>
> (*Æneid* XII, 436–40)

compare:

> My Son, from my Example learn the War, ⎫
> In Camps to suffer, and in Fields to dare: ⎬
> But happier Chance than mine attend thy care. ⎭

> This Day my hand thy tender Age shall shield,
> And crown with Honours of the conquer'd Field:
> Thou, when thy riper Years shall send thee forth,
> To toils of War, be mindful of my Worth:
> Assert thy birthright; and in Arms be known,
> For *Hector*'s nephew, and *Æneas* son.
>
> (XII, 644–52; *Works*, VI, 784–5)

Setting annotated parallel texts against an imitation or a classic translation in order to generate critical comparisons is not aimed at judging the latter, but at reflecting the twin locations of the text and the translator/reader. Any translation is an act of choice, with voices, ambiguities, ironies, and subtexts suppressed or made explicit, with new English associations and resonances created. The question above, of what voice Dryden gave Æneas, is a question about the implications of his interpretation of Æneas as *exemplum* compared to a twenty-first century reading of Æneas. It may be that a student sees Dryden as suppressing the 'pessimistic' voice of Æneas. If so, that points to a crux in the text that Dryden as poet-creator needed to solve in his translation, and sends readers back to the glossed text to generate their own interpretative solutions.

Using an annotated literal translation next to a classic poetic translation is in fact to make pedagogic use of Dryden's categories of translation (in the Preface to *Ovid's Epistles*, *Poems*, I, 384–5):

1. *Metaphrase*: 'turning an author word by word';
2. *Paraphrase*: 'translation with latitude, where the author is kept in view ... so as never to be lost, but his words are not so strictly followed as his sense; and that too is admitted to be amplified, but not altered';
3. *Imitation*: where 'the translator (if now he has not lost that name) assumes the liberty, not only to vary from the words and sense, but to forsake them both as he sees the occasion'.

Dryden had a clear sense of the different purposes, as well as categories, of translation. The making of such distinctions is perhaps even more important today, when series of classics in English publish every kind of translation indifferently. Such series of 'translations' do not locate themselves against Dryden's distinctions, do not declare their relationship with the original text. They lead to the textually uncritical study of 'classics in translation' rather than the critical understanding that comes from the comparative study of 'classics through translations'. 'Classics in translation' courses are usually seen as secondary to 'real' Classics courses, in that Classics students study the 'real' text. This presupposes that Classics students read classical languages as if they were their mother tongue, read classical texts as if they were their native literature – without needing to translate. This is a myth, and it does no harm to stress that translation is an achieved act of interpretation incumbent on the most fluent of linguists. However, Classics in translation is all too often only that – the study of the translated texts rather than the study of the problematics of translating classic, alien texts. All too often Classics in translation treats the translation uncritically, as if it were simply the original.

Forming a reading of a classical text in the twenty-first century is for anybody a kind of journey across alien ground. 'Metaphrase' can be used to suggest a journey using scaffolding to get across the text, scaffolding which provides footholds but shows the text beneath. Unlike the pejorative associations of the 'crib' – a tool for the lazy which leads to dependence – I see metaphrase as positively encouraging language work because it constantly shows the structures and fabric of the original text and encourages progressively sophisticated reference to it. I use texts with the crucial words untranslated – a literal text of Virgil with words such as *virtus*, *pius*/*pietas*, *furor*, left in Latin.

'Paraphrase' is potentially the most dangerous of the three methods, as apparently offering to follow the contours of the text beneath, but at an accessible level – dangerous because it implies a magical transformation of the text beneath. It implies, that is, that the alien can be fully transformed, not just brought into dialogue. Paraphrase offers a firm, single-planed landscape. But classical texts are anything but single-planed – in artistry, complexity, or voice. They are in complex dialogue with the past; they have provoked the greatest of poets into engagement with them. As classicists we do ourselves a disservice if we imply that, with scholarship, the text can so easily be unrolled and traversed. Rather, it is the knots, provocations, difficulties, challenges explored or silenced in translations through the ages and needing to be explored again in ours, that make our texts classic.

And so I come to 'imitation' – imaged as a new landscape in vital relationship with, but different from, the ground of the text beneath. Imitation (a category that includes many classic translations, in that they have permitted themselves the liberty of expanding, updating, and reflecting on the text) constantly demands of readers that they question the relationship of the text to the imitation, and invites critical appreciation of both. Such questioning produces insights into verbal or structural features of the text which the act of translation reveals are under strain. Imitation can also offer the result of the author/translator's wrestling with the issues and cruxes of the text.[8] The result of the wrestling will be a deeper engagement with the text. In places, the only way to shift the burden of the author from one's shoulders may well be to take upon oneself the decision of issues in the text, making the text one's own by resolving a question, or suppressing an ambiguity or a dissenting voice.

In using annotated metaphrase and parallel texts I present the student with a translated text whose surface is disturbed by references, transliterated key words, and so on. Such a text stresses that the work of translation in its largest sense is the reader's: that translation is an act of interpretation, of intercultural communication, a work in progress and not a new, definitive text. This is the opposite of regarding the translated text as what 'if [the poet] were living, and an Englishman ... he would probably have written'.

The distinction is subtle but important. A Homer writing in the seventeenth or eighteenth century might, for example, see a code of honour as an absolute claim upon upon a 'gentleman'. But a glossed text of Homer's *Iliad* shows a coordinating cluster of words with claims that are dramatized and problematized in and by the various characters' speeches. The Greek words can be translated into contemporary English, but they then bring with them contemporary associations and status. They become part of a code of honour implied to be as stable in Homer's society as in Dryden's or Pope's. But the *Iliad* is made up of claims and counter-claims – it opens with the dispute over the right of Agamemnon and then Achilles to a piece of *geras*, the prize or reward for heroic acts. Achilles says that Agamemnon has perverted the whole 'heroic system' – that heroes gain *kleos* ('everlasting reputation in song'), *timê* (heroic 'ranking', 'honour'), and the material correlates of *timê*: *geras* in the form of spoil, prizes, rewards, all in exchange for exertion, danger, and death on the battlefield. He can and will no longer fight: a position argued over from various perspectives for most of the Book. The heroic position is explained by Sarpedon:

> Glaucus, why is it you and I are given *timê* before others in Lykia,
> and all men look upon us as if we were immortals ... ?
> Therefore we must stand in the forefront of the Lykians
> and bear our part of the blazing of battle,
> so that a man of the close-armoured Lykians may say of us:
> Indeed these are not without *kleos*, these lords of ours ...
> Man, supposing you and I, escaping this battle,
> would be able to live on forever, ageless, immortal,
> so neither would I myself go on fighting in the foremost
> nor would I urge you into the fighting where men win *kudos*.

But now, seeing the *kêres* [spirits of death] stand close about us
in their thousands, no man can turn aside nor escape them,
let us go on and win the *euchos* [victory shout] for ourselves or
yield it to others.[9]

Pope's version is splendid: a heroic declaration of the manly courage that
(in Homer's Greek lines here) inspired the dying statesman, Lord
Granville, and 'recalled to his mind the distinguishing part he had taken
in pubic affairs':[10]

> Why boast we, *Glaucus!* our extended Reign,
> Where *Xanthus'* Streams enrich the *Lycian* Plain ...
> Why on those Shores are we with Joy survey'd,
> Admir'd as Heroes, and as Gods obey'd?
> Unless great Acts superior Merit prove,
> And vindicate the bount'ous Pow'rs above.
> 'Tis ours, the Dignity they give, to grace;
> The first in Valour, as the first in Place;
> That when with wond'ring Eyes our martial Bands
> Behold our Deeds transcending our Commands,
> Such, they may cry, deserve the sov'reign State,
> Whom those that envy, dare not imitate!
> Could all our Care elude the gloomy Grave,
> Which claims no less the fearful than the brave,
> For Lust of Fame I should not vainly dare
> In fighting Fields, nor urge thy Soul to War.
> But since, alas! ignoble Age must come,
> Disease, and Death's inexorable Doom;
> The Life which others pay, let us bestow,
> And give to Fame what we to Nature owe;
> Brave tho' we fall, and honour'd if we live,
> Or let us Glory gain, or Glory give![11]

'Glory' has an emotive force and transcendent appeal that 'battle victory
shout' does not; the literal battlefield ('since the *kêres* are all around') has
been turned to a metaphor of the human condition ('ignoble Age ...
Disease'). The centre of the poem is inspired by a kind of *noblesse oblige*:
'The Life which others pay, let us bestow'; a hierarchy divinely blessed,
'bounteous Pow'rs', 'grace'. There is a soulful negativity worthy of A. E.
Housman about 'gloomy Grave', a levelling in death of 'no less the
fearful than the brave'. And the final, tremendous call to arms is very
different from Sarpedon's understanding that since the only immortality

available is esteem from colleagues and the poet, they have no option but to re-enter the killing field in order to either claim a victory or add to someone else's score.

The difference is not one of meaning but of normative value; the vocabulary is equivalent but not equal in effect or in univocality. If Sarpedon can inspire Glaucus, as Homer inspired Lord Granville, then they and all the other heroes have access to something worth fighting and dying for. But if each hero has to consider for himself whether the 'heroic exchange' of esteem and prizes for painful effort and death is worth it, there is an ever-present uncertainty. The tragic possibility is constantly available, that *timê* and *kleos* might be worth nothing rather than everything. By keeping such words untranslated, the reader of a glossed metaphrase version has constantly to ask what value is being accorded them in this speech, in this context. Once translated into a heroic English vocabulary, they acquire a fixed price: words such as 'renown', 'honour', 'fame', and 'grace' come trailing clouds of glory.

The continuous and difficult task of reader and translator is to discriminate between judgements within the text and judgements made by the reader out of engagement with the character. This is a particularly nice problem, involving as it does an assessment of the evaluative vocabulary of the various voices in the text. When Dryden talks of Virgil changing 'the manners of Homer's heroes in his *Aeneis* ... and for the better. For Virgil's Age was more civilized, and better bred', his language is overtly judgemental (though it is to be noted that his attitude changed when he actually came to work on his translation of Homer, as did Chapman's ideal of the classical 'Stoic hero' by which he initially judged Odysseus, Achilles, and Hector, under the pressure of his engagement with the text).

Central to the *Iliad*, needless to say, is the evaluation of Achilles as a hero. Much is said in the text about his psychology and state of mind; in Book XXI, when he is engaged in an orgy of killing after the death of Patroclus, there is a highly charged piece of direct speech. Lykaon, whom he had before spared, appeals for mercy, arguing that he should be spared as a *xenos* (someone who had once been a member of Achilles' household, albeit as a prisoner) and as a suppliant. Lykaon

> heard the voice [of Achilles] without pity:
> '*Nêpie*, no longer speak to me of ransom, nor argue it.
> In the time before Patroclus came to his day of destiny
> Then it was the way of my heart's choice to be sparing ...
> Now there is not one Trojan who can escape death ...
> So *phile*, you die also. Why all this clamour?

> Patroclus also is dead, who was better by far than you are.
> Do you not see what a man I am? ...
> Yet even I have also my death and my strong destiny ...'
>   (XXI, 98–110, Lattimore translation, adapted)

The tone of this is difficult yet essential to determine. The passage brings to a head many issues in the *Iliad* (which is introduced as being about the wrath of Achilles and about the many deaths of heroes that resulted); Achilles is here marked as having moved away from what has been set up as the heroic norm, both in not respecting claims that he used to and in taking a pragmatic view of life and death. The question of the presentation of Achilles' voice and how it reflects on the more usual 'heroic' battleground encounters sharpens the issues of the text as a whole. It is also an important passage in that it can be taken as simple only if it is read as espousing a simple attitude: either that war is a senseless bloodbath, or that there is a noble heroism that Achilles embodies – that in the face of death he is a hero preeminent. Readings not pushing the sentiment to those extremes make the passage a problematizing statement of the human condition.

In seminars I first of all get students to work on the passage in glossed translation: to read it to one another, seeing what and how many voices they can generate for Achilles: sadistic? cold? insanely angry? philosophical? sardonic? gently sad? The resulting readings tend to centre on the tone of the two glossed words – *nêpie*, a 'narratorial' word often translated as 'poor fool', used to denote a limitation on the understanding of the addressee; and *phile*, 'friend', arguably either sarcastic or denoting a commonality between them despite their apparently distinct status. Both words are open to various interpretations in the Greek: *nêpios* when used outside speech is a rare mark of the narratorial voice, indicating the mismatch between the judgement of the character and that of the poet. A particularly dramatic example is Homer's comment on Andromache preparing the bath for Hektor who is already dead: *nêpios* (XXII, 445). Here it may privilege the focalization of Achilles, implying that like the poet he sees beyond the 'heroic condition'; like the poet, his viewpoint is distanced from the ordinary human and heroic perception of Lykaon.

Philos must also carry a basic conversational meaning, denoting merely 'the one addressed'. Lykaon has appealed to a stronger bond than that of addressee: he speaks as a *xenos* and as a suppliant. Though denying those claims, Achilles' whole speech invites Lykaon to acknowledge the other bonds between them. It is for the addressee outside the text to weigh the levels of irony in play – ideally in dialogue with the text and with other readers, past and present.

If one turns to Pope's translation of the passage, one finds it to be comparatively univocal:

> Talk not of Life, or Ransom, (he replies)
> *Patroclus* dead, whoever meets me, dies:
> In vain a single *Trojan* sues for Grace;
> But least, the Sons of *Priam*'s hateful Race.
> Die then, my Friend! what boots it to deplore?
> The great, the good *Patroclus* is no more!
> He, far thy Better, was fore-doom'd to die,
> "And thou, dost thou bewail Mortality?"
> See'st thou not me, whom Nature's Gifts adorn,
> Sprung from a Hero, from a Goddess born;
> The Day shall come (which nothing can avert)
> When by the Spear, the Arrow, or the Dart,
> By Night, or Day, by Force or by Design,
> Impending Death and certain Fate are mine.
> Die then—He said; and as the Word he spoke
> The fainting Stripling sunk, before the Stroke[12]

The horror is muted by the inevitability of the completing 'stroke'; the measured couplets lend an air of reasonableness and self-control to the potentially demented speech. Only one of the two words that were the key to the various readings is retained here: *nêpios*, that mark of difference in consciousness between narrator, focalizer, and reader, disappears altogether. *Philos* is retained, but is rendered univocal by its context. Achilles in Pope's translation has faced squarely the human condition and can condemn Lykaon for not so doing.

This episode is woven by Virgil into the heart of the structure of *Æneid* X, the Book with which I started this paper as being one in which any translator must feel the 'weight of the whole Author' upon him. Here, issues of Homeric allusion, *pietas*, and the cost of *imperium* come to a head, and pose crucial questions for translator and reader alike. (The episode is interwoven with that of Lausus and Mezentius: the latter's lament was memorably translated by Dryden in his *Æneis*, X, 1206–22.)

In Book X Æneas slaughters the enemy, overtaken by *furor* at the death of his young companion Pallas. Virgil subtly refashions the Lykaon material. Æneas speaks to the supplicating Magus; Magus, like Lykaon, appeals to the values that obtained before Æneas' young companion was killed:

By the shades of your father and by the hopes you have of Iulus ...
I beg you to spare this life of mine for the sake of my son and my
    father ...
I have talents of ... silver and ... gold.

                                                              (X, ´524–7)

Magus, in a foreshadowing of the final appeal of Turnus at the end of the
epic, appeals to the world outside, the world of benefits, of rational
decisions: 'Not on me does the victory of the Trojans turn, nor will one
life make such a difference' (X, 528–9). Æneas responds: 'Turnus did
away with such *belli commercia* when Pallas was killed' (X, 532–3).
Æneas, like Achilles, replies that conditions have changed. But Achilles
explains that what has changed is his perception of the heroic and human
condition. Æneas however is blunt and curt; ignoring the absolute claim
of the suppliant, he dispatches him while he is still supplicating (X, 537–
41). His brusqueness here cuts short the expectation of a fitting reply to
Magus, an expectation in part created by the intertextuality. (The insight
into the emotional and psychological state of the protagonist given in
Achilles' reply to Lykaon is deferred from the Magus to the Lausus
incident later in Book X.) The reply we might expect would be just not
only to the widening of the focus from epic-heroic to human, but also in
providing an insight parallel to that of Achilles' reply to Lykaon. Both
expectations are unfulfilled as, raging (*furit*, 545), he goes straight on to
kill another suppliant. He threatens him with the fate with which
Achilles threatened Lykaon – to lie unburied while the fish nibble his
wounds (X, 560). For the rest of Book X Æneas is a battle-machine, his
mental state revealed only in his actions. Virgil has retained the battle
madness of Achilles, but refashioned it into the subtly different *furor*.

    Achilles in the *Iliad* is frequently referred to as battle-mad, *memaôs*,
but so too are other fighters.[13] Æneas in this Book is in the grip of *furor*
(604); the others that also *furire* are demented, victims of supernatural
forces.[14] Æneas is a different kind of hero from Achilles; he carries, *inter
alia*, Roman obligations and Stoic expectations upon him: he is
preeminently *pius*. But he is also *furens*: to be *furens*, unlike being *memaôs*,
is connected with irrational or unconsidered judgements;[15] to be out of
control of one's rational powers. Æneas was overtaken by *furor* in the fall
of Troy, where he would have stayed to fight and forgo his destiny (II,
316), and in the battle after Pallas is killed, as discussed above. Elsewhere
he has a furious mind (*furiata mens*); crucially and perhaps ambiguously
in the last scene of the epic, he is fired by *furiae* when he kills Turnus
(XII, 946).

    Virgil, as any translator must, has rendered the psychology of the

Iliad into the value system of his own age. But in so doing, again like any translator, he has translated the action of the protagonist into a system whereby he can be judged. He has also given Æneas the preeminent quality of the value system into which he has been translated: he is *pius*, as well as *furens*. But this translation brings with it a frame of judgement: to be *furens* and *pius*, unlike being *memaôs*, is potentially to be at fault.

The second part of the Lykaon incident, the speech to the victim, is deferred by Virgil until the end of the Book. In between, Æneas kills *furens*, but is again and again called *pius*, even when collecting victims for human sacrifice. These would seem to be contradictory qualities, the one appropriate to a Homeric, individualist hero, the other to the forebear of Rome. Virgil's hero is a creative refashioning of Homeric heroism for a different society; a hero who however is not free from the material from which he is fashioned. He has Homeric experiences but carries a burden of responsibility to his son's and Rome's future. He is a vehicle as well as an individual. *Pietas*, perhaps translating for Roman society the value of *aidôs* in the *Iliad*, demands acknowledgement of family and sacred duties and then appropriate action. This preeminent quality is shown to be far more than simple 'piety' by being applied to Æneas even when killing a priest (X, 591). In previous Books, *furor* has been opposed to *pietas*, denoting Æneas' loss of *pietas*, his forgetting his duty to Anchises, Iulus, and posterity (e.g. in Troy, II, 316). *Furor* has marked him as being overtaken by individualist, heroic, Homeric tendencies; *pietas* as respecting the claims of his dependants and posterity. In the 200 lines between the two incidents that together transpose the Lykaon story, attention is called to the strain between the two values of *pietas* and *furor*: a strain that correlates to the strains upon Æneas imposed by the values both of the *Iliad* and of Augustus. Virgil is hence calling attention to the strain on every poet/translator, who necessarily creates in one culture while in vital relationship with the culture as well as the spirit of the original.

In the concluding transposition of the Lykaon scene, the dramatic possiblities of the translator's double allegiance, of the translation's double resonance, are felt. Æneas is still *pius* (783) and still raging (*furit*, 802). At 811–12, demented, full of savage anger, he taunts his young opponent Lausus with ... *pietas*. Lausus has been accorded narratorial sympathy; his *pietas* for his evil father may be misplaced, but the taunt and his brutal killing seem to place Æneas' heroic qualities under strain. As at the killing of Lykaon in the *Iliad*, this is the moment when the human cost of heroic action, to victor as well as victim, is felt by audience and Æneas alike:

the point going straight through his light shield, no proper armour
to match the threats he had uttered. It pierced, too, the tunic his
mother had woven for him with a soft thread of gold and filled the
folds of it with blood. Then did his life leave his body and go in
sorrow through the air to join the shades. But when Aeneas, son of
Anchises, saw the dying face and features, the face strangely white,
he groaned from his heart in pity and held out his hand, as there
came into his mind the thought of his own *pietas* for his father, and
he said: 'What will the *pius* Aeneas now give to match such merit?
... In your misfortune you will have one consolation for your cruel
death, that you fell by the hand of the great Aeneas.'[16]

'What will *pius* Æneas now give to match such merit?' It is a remarkably
direct question; it is, remarkably, a direct question. Æneas speaks the
epitaph of Lausus out loud. As he does so, the epitaph becomes part of
the *Æneid* and gains the immortality it promises; Æneas' direct speech is
self-fulfilling. The immortality is that valued and offered in the Homeric
world of the hero. The immortality achieved is the *kleos*, the eternal fame
on the lips of the bard, that Sarpedon speaks of to Glaucus. At this
moment what is offered is a Homeric allusion, a self-conscious claim to
be an epic hero while offering the consolation 'You're history!' Æneas in
this passage is in and out of time; he is also claiming to be in two times:
the *kleos*-giving Homeric past and the *pietas*-valuing Augustan future.
This mirrors the time-span of those attributes: *kleos* transmits from the
past and promises for the future; *pietas* respects the claims of both the
past (Troy, Anchises) and the future (Iulus and the Iulii). But the
immediacy of the emotion, the immediacy of the expression, undercuts
the timelessness promised. Now *pius* Æneas offers the only consolation –
'that you fell by the hand of the great Æneas'. Whether this Homeric
consolation is adequate the words 'infelix' ('tragically unlucky' – like
Dido and Pallas) and 'miseram mortem' ('cruel death') seem to doubt.
Æneas, by naming himself with his stock, already ironized, epithet, is
made to seem to reflect on his epic status.

    Virgil has transposed the potential multivocality of the Lykaon speech
into a variously-voiced series of indicators of Æneas' psychology. The
strain on him to fulfil two sorts of definition of heroism – the *pietas*-
regarding Roman and the individualistic epic hero, fighting *furens*, lost in
the moment, has been suggested. Both values have been problematized
for Æneas, as 'heroic' values were problematized for Achilles. They have
also been problematized for the reader, entering into dialogue both with
Æneas and with an Æneas in dialogue with Achilles. The problematization
continues to the end of the later epic: the *Iliad* ends with Achilles

Teaching Troubling Texts

acceding to Priam's supplication, the *Æneid* with Æneas, fired by *furiis*, refusing Turnus' supplication and killing him. The allusivity of the scene renders the ending problematic, renders the closure partial and disturbing.

I started with Dryden's translation of this passage, and with a question: whether it matters that Dryden, in his achingly affecting rendering, changed Æneas' direct question to a rhetorical one. Many have found Virgil's voice to be prevailingly plangent, best expressed in Æneas' own words when surveying the representation of his story in art at I, 462:

> sunt lacrimae rerum et mentem mortalia tangunt
>
> (Tears in the nature of things, mens' minds touched by human mortality)

Dryden the poet has emulated that voice, has with his poesie indeed opened Virgil's poesie. But in so doing he has suppressed other voices – Æneas', and, behind that, Achilles'. He cuts out the epithet and question ('What will *pius* Æneas now give to match such merit?'), and ends the speech with a resounding sentiment rather than a troubling question. In recasting the openness at the end into closure, Dryden has rendered univocal what Virgil made complex.

When Dryden made his translation he creatively refashioned his material, including the values and ideals of the text, for a different age; Virgil refashioned and reconceptualized Homer in such a way. The question to be asked about any such refashioning is whether it could be said that, in Dryden's terms, it transfuses the values and ideals of the previous text or continues in dialogue with them. Whatever our judgement, the point is in any case made, that using a metaphrastic glossed text, with associations and intertextualities marked, next to a great translation, opens up a dialogue between readers and poetic translators. Dryden would surely have been pleased that his great work should be used to raise the whole question of what it is to be in dialogue with the literary texts of a great yet distant culture: another 'Giant Race before the Flood'.

NOTES

1. Virgil is quoted throughout from one of the editions used by Dryden, de la Rue's *P. Virgilii Maronis Opera interpretatione et notis illustravit Carolus Ruaeus*, second edition (Paris, 1682).
2. 'Epistle to the Reader', 142, *Homer's Iliads* (1611); *Chapman's Homer*, edited by Allardyce Nicoll, 2 vols (New York, 1956), I, 10.

3. 'Graecia capta ferum victorem cepit' (Horace *Ep*. II.i, 156).
4. 'Discourse Concerning the Original and Progress of Satire', *Poems*, III, 433.
5. *Æneid* XII, 435–40; Ruaeus, p. 841.
6. H. D. Jocelyn argues that in Accius' version these lines may have been spoken by an Ajax going out to war rather than about to commit suicide. See 'Ancient Scholarship and Virgil's Use of Republican Latin Poetry, II', *Classical Quarterly*, 15 (1965), 126–44 (pp. 127–9).
7. 'To Sir *Richard Fanshaw* upon his Translation of *Pastor Fido*', ll. 9–10, 15–16, 23–4; *Poetical Works of Sir John Denham*, edited by Theodore Howard Banks, second edition (Hamden, CT, 1969), pp. 143–4.
8. Dryden was worried at the prospect of translating the whole of the *Æneid*, as he had previously only translated texts that 'had most affected [him] in the reading', and through which he could give himself and find himself. Now he had to grapple with the 'weight of a whole Author', with all that author's complexity and design. The point is made by David Hopkins, *John Dryden* (Cambridge, 1986), p. 157; the quotation is from the *Dedication of the Æneis*.
9. XII, 310–28, adapted from Richmond Lattimore's translation *The Iliad of Homer* (Chicago, 1951; hereafter 'Lattimore').
10. For Granville see Matthew Arnold, 'On Translating Homer' in *Matthew Arnold: On the Classical Tradition*, edited by R. H. Super (Ann Arbor, 1960), pp. 97–216 (p. 108).
11. Lines 371–2, 377–96; *The Twickenham Edition of the Works of Alexander Pope*, VIII: *The Iliad of Homer, Books X–XXIV*, edited by Maynard Mack (London, 1967), pp. 95–6.
12. Lines 111–26; *The Twickenham Pope*, VIII, 426.
13. *Memaôs/emmemaôs* (XX, 284, 468; XXI, 174); but the word is also applied to his opponents (XX, 386, 400). It is in the direct speech to Lykaon that the clearest, or perhaps most multi-faceted, view is given of his psychological state. He has before killed or ransomed according to whim or pride. He is now full of *menos*, eager to kill (XXI, 33, 170, 176). He is like an inhuman fire in his raging (*anamaimaei*, XX, 490) to win *kudos* (XX, 502), to make all Trojans pay for the death of Patroclus (XXI, 134). Is this battle-fury culpable or a mark of his heroic stature? The Scamander upbraids him for his excess and his cruelty, but, as with the interchange with Lykaon, whenever he is addressed he answers rationally. There seems to be no suggestion that he is demented rather than in a proper fighting state.
14. Dido (IV, 65, 101, 298, 465ff.) and Turnus (IX, 760) are also subject to *furor* – Dido is out of her mind, a victim of Juno and Amor (IV, 91); Turnus together with Amata is a victim of the Fury Allecto (VII, 456–66). Only in Æneas does the *furor* seem to be internally generated.
15. See Francis Cairns, *Vergil's Augustan Epic* (Cambridge, 1989), pp. 83–5 (in the *Georgics* it was the force that made Orpheus turn and look back).
16. *Æneid* X, 815–30; adapted from *The Aeneid*, translated by David West (Harmondsworth, 1990), p. 268.

Augustan Dryden

Robin Sowerby

In the frontispiece to Dryden's 1697 volume *The Works of Virgil in English* (Figure 1), Apollo, the god of poetry itself, confers his laurel upon Virgil, book in hand, and eyes cast up to the heavens. He gazes at a small cherub directing our attention to Dryden's Virgil enclosed in a design with a motif that provides a visual echo of the poet's laureate wreath. The spectators' eyes are drawn to the triangle at the top of the plate in which Dryden's name, closely followed by that of the publisher Jacob Tonson, is at the apex. The plate makes discreet but clear claims for the Dryden translation it introduces. Tonson's marketing instincts have been well vindicated: 300 years later this plate served as a highly appropriate emblem for the University of Bristol conference celebrating Dryden as poet, classicist, and translator. The idea embodied in the image is a very powerful one not just for what it might claim for Dryden's Virgil which it is advertising, nor even for what it might suggest about the centrality of his translating activity in the ordinary meaning of the phrase, but because it is the visual equivalent of the claim that Dryden himself makes for his wider contribution to English poetry in his 'Postscript to the Reader': that the art of poetry has been successfully translated by way of Virgil into English.

Whatever the truth of that, it marks out, more successfully than any other visual image available, Dryden's ideal relation to the classical tradition. I mean by this it defines his relation to the poets of Augustan Rome as it may be thought Dryden himself would have been pleased to define it. The former Laureate of England is put beside (or above) the uncrowned laureate of Rome. Horace, of course, is equally a laureate poet, and, as a critic, the great vindicator and asserter of Augustan artistic values. But in the generic hierarchy, lyric is inferior to epic, and as an hexameter poet Horace works in the inferior genres of satire and the verse epistle. Although Horace is an Augustan refiner of Lucilius, it is Virgil's Augustan refinement of previous practitioners like Ennius and Lucretius that establishes the norms for Augustan hexameter practice in high and dignified narrative. Virgil's practice in the three genres in which he worked, pastoral, georgic, and epic, represented in the Renaissance and beyond the highest embodiment of the Augustan ideals

Figure 1. *Frontispiece of The Works of Virgil in English*, 1697.

of refinement, urbanity, and poise that are the desiderata of Horace in his literary epistles. As for Ovid, a later Augustan who eschewed the laureate role and fell foul of Augustus, there is no doubt that Dryden felt a close poetical affinity with him, but equally that it was an affinity which Dryden also felt the need to resist.

In the 'Postscript' to his Virgil translation, two comparisons are implied between the Roman poet and his English translator. Dryden begins by drawing a distinction between his own position, sadly marginalized under an uncongenial government, and the happy ideal of Virgil's position, feted and honoured in the reign of Augustus. But he goes on to use the occasion of his translation to make a claim to fame that contains an implicit comparison in their poetic achievements:

> For, what I have done, Imperfect as it is, for want of Health and leisure to Correct it, will be judg'd in after Ages, and possibly in the present, to be no dishonour to my Native Country; whose Language and Poetry wou'd be more esteem'd abroad, if they were better understood. Somewhat (give me leave to say) I have added to both of them in the choice of Words, and Harmony of Numbers, which were wanting, especially the last, in all our Poets, even in those who being endu'd with Genius, yet have not Cultivated their Mother-Tongue with sufficient Care; or relying on the Beauty of their Thoughts, have judg'd the Ornament of Words, and sweetness of Sound unnecessary.
>
> (*Works*, VI, 807)

The comparison implicit here, implicit to the point of being almost buried, points not to difference but to similarity; both poets in their attention to metre and diction have cultivated and refined native poetic practice. This is the Augustan affinity which I shall be talking about in this paper; I am using 'Augustan' as an aesthetic term without regard to any of its political associations, and seek to demonstrate by juxtaposing the mature Dryden with the early Augustan Denham that this refinement is achieved by the systematic application of artistic principles and techniques supremely embodied in the poetry of Virgil.

Allusion to Virgil is a constant thread throughout Dryden's career. His reading and study of Virgil must have begun well before that career started, when he encountered Virgil in his education at Westminster school. A grammar-school boy in the seventeenth century cut his poetic teeth on the Latin classics. If he composed Latin verse in his advanced years there, as is most likely, Virgil would have been the chief authority for classical practice in hexameter poetry, just as Cicero has always

represented the norm for classical Latin prose. I am not aware of any
direct evidence for Dryden's practice in the art of Latin verse
composition at school or university, but one Latin poem survives from
his early career,[1] and the following extract from his Preface to *Albion and
Albanius* of 1685 suggests that he was well grounded in the basic
technicalities of the craft:

> 'Tis no easy matter in our Language to make words so smooth, and
> numbers so harmonious, that they shall almost set themselves, and
> yet there are rules for this in nature: and as great a certainty of
> quantity in our Syllables, as either in the *Greek* or the *Latin:* But
> let Poets and Judges understand those first, and then let them
> begin to study *English* ... The chief secret is in the choice of
> Words; and by this choice I do not here mean Elegancy of
> expression, but propriety of sound to be varied according to the
> Nature of the Subject. Perhaps a time may come, when I may treat
> of this more largely, out of some Observations which I have made
> from *Homer* and *Virgil*, who amongst all the Poets, only understood
> the Art of Numbers, and of that which was properly call'd
> *Rhythmus* by the Ancients.
>
> (*Works*, XV, 9–10)

This is a promise he never fulfilled.

The mention of *rhythmus* here leads me to broach the question of
rhyme. In its refined Augustan form, the English rhyming couplet has its
own dynamic which is distinct from that of the periodic style of the
Latin hexameter as perfected by Virgil. It has sometimes been said that
this distinctive development of the English heroic precludes any classical
influence, or that if influence is to be claimed, it must come by way of
the Latin elegiac couplet. It is true that the first couplets of any quality
in English to show the distinctive rhetorical patterning, with a tendency
to closure, that became the practice of the later Augustans are those
crafted by Marlowe in his translations of Ovid's elegies. But the Latin
elegiac, though predominantly closed, is not actually very like the
English heroic in its overall movement. This may be suggested by
Coleridge's representation of it:

> In the hexameter rises the fountain's silvery column;
> In the pentameter aye falling in melody back.[2]

Secondly, the rhythmic regularity of the Latin hexameter ending, where
the fifth foot is always a dactyl and the sixth foot never a dactyl (there is

only the very occasional exception to this rule), provides the recurring effect of a regularly rising rhythm, tum-ti-ti-tum-tum, that is analogous to the effect of rhyme, and indeed described as such by some early commentators on Virgil. So analogies are indeed possible between the English heroic and the Latin hexameter. Finally, perhaps in response to what Milton seems to say about rhyme and ancient liberty in the headnote to his second edition of *Paradise Lost* (1674),[3] Dryden provides in his poem to Roscommon an energetic defence, distinguishing between bad and good practice in rhyming. Cultured song, he explains, was first translated from Greece to Rome,

> Till barb'rous nations, and more barb'rous times,
> Debas'd the majesty of verse to rhymes:
> Those rude at first, a kind of hobbling prose
> That limped along, and tinkled in the close;
> But Italy, reviving from the trance
> Of Vandal, Goth, and monkish ignorance,
> With pauses, cadence, and well-vowelled words,
> And all the graces a good ear affords,
> Made rhyme an art; and Dante's polish'd page
> Restored a silver, not a golden age.
> Then Petrarch followed, and in him we see   ⎫
> What rhyme improved in all its height can be: ⎬
> At best a pleasing sound, and fair barbarity.[4] ⎭

Out of context, this last line might suggest that the most artful rhyme remains barbarous. But in the context of the overall argument defending the art of rhyme, the emphasis must fall upon the fairness of the barbarity: that is, beautiful things may have barbarous origins, and the barbarous origin does not preclude the possibility of beauty.

We would expect Dryden to be an enthusiastic proponent of the virtues of the poets he chose to translate. But no reader of his criticism from the introduction to *Annus Mirabilis* to the *Dedication of the Æneis* could fail to be impressed by the cogency of his appeal to Virgil as model and authority, and by the frequency of his allusions to Virgil both in his poetry and prose. Moreover, the allusions in his prose are often very specific, and might sometimes be called exercises in practical criticism. He has more to say in a practical way of Virgil than of any other poet ancient or modern. Here is a selection of Dryden's pronouncements on Virgil, starting with some general remarks, going on to versification, then to diction, and finally to the figures, before coming back again to a final general consideration.

I drew my definition of poetical wit from my particular consideration of him, for propriety of thoughts and words are only to be found in him ... This exact propriety of Virgil I particularly regarded as a great part of his character.

> (Preface to *Sylvae*, *Poems*, II, 242–3)

my chief Ambition is to please those Readers, who have discernment enough to prefer *Virgil* before any other Poet in the *Latine* Tongue. Such Spirits as he desir'd to please, such wou'd I chuse for my Judges, and wou'd stand or fall by them alone.

> (*Dedication of the Æneis*, *Works*, V, 326)

Long before I undertook this Work, I was no stranger to the Original. I had also studied *Virgil*'s Design, his disposition of it, his Manners, his judicious management of the Figures, the sober retrenchments of his Sense, which always leaves somewhat to gratifie our imagination, on which it may enlarge at pleasure; but above all, the Elegance of his Expressions, and the harmony of his Numbers.

> (*Dedication of the Æneis*, *Works*, V, 326)

His verse is everywhere sounding the very thing in your ears whose sense it bears; yet the numbers are perpetually varied, to increase the delight of the reader; so that the same sounds are never repeated twice together ... Ovid with all his sweetness, has as little variety of numbers and sound as he.

> (Preface to *Sylvae*, *Poems*, II, 241–2)

The turns of his verse, his breakings, his propriety, his numbers and his gravity I have as far imitated as the poverty of our language and the hastiness of my performance would allow.

> (Preface to *Sylvae*, *Poems*, II, 244)

His words are not only chosen, but the places in which he ranks them for the sound; he who removes them from the Station wherein their Master sets them, spoils the Harmony. What he says of the *Sibyls* Prophecies, may be as properly apply'd to every word of his: They must be read, in order as they lie; the least breath discomposes them, and somewhat of their Divinity is lost. I cannot boast that I have been thus exact in my Verses, but I have endeavour'd to follow the example of my Master: and am the first *Englishman*, perhaps, who made it his design to copy him in his

Numbers, his choice of Words, and his placing them for the sweetness of the sound.

(Dedication of the Æneis, Works, V, 319)

We have the Proverb, *manum de tabulâ*, from the Painters; which signifies, to know when to give over, and to lay by the Pencil. Both *Homer* and *Virgil* practis'd this Precept wonderfully well, but *Virgil* the better of the two.

('A Parallel Betwixt Poetry and Painting', *Works*, XX, 75–6)

But two particular lines in 'Mezentius and Lausus' I cannot so easily excuse; they are indeed remotely allied to Virgil's sense, but they are too like the trifling tenderness of Ovid ... :
When Lausus died, I was already slain.
This appears pretty enough at first sight, but I am convinced for many reasons that the expression is too bold, that Virgil would not have said it, though Ovid would.

(Preface to *Sylvae, Poems*, II, 245)

He is everywhere above conceits of epigrammatic wit and gross hyperboles: he maintains majesty in the midst of plainness; he shines, but glares not, and is stately without ambition, which is the vice of Lucan.

(Preface to *Sylvae, Poems*, II, 242)

Strong and glowing Colours are the just resemblances of bold Metaphors, but both must be judiciously apply'd; for there is a difference betwixt daring and foolhardiness. *Lucan* and *Statius* often ventured them too far, our *Virgil* never.

('A Parallel Betwixt Poetry and Painting', *Works*, XX, 73)

There was an *Ennius,* and in process of Time a *Lucilius,* and a *Lucretius,* before *Virgil* and *Horace;* even after *Chaucer* there was a *Spencer,* a *Harrington,* a *Fairfax,* before *Waller* and *Denham* were in being: And our Numbers were in their Nonage till these last appear'd.

(Preface to the *Fables*, Kinsley, IV, 1453)

Although Dryden's response to the political aspects of the Augustan age changed with time and with his own experience as English Laureate, his Augustan aesthetic suffered no reversals from the moment in his career when he embraced it in rejecting the metaphysical tendencies of his youth, to the very end, when, having translated Virgil, he consciously went beyond it in the *Fables*. Even when he transgressed it, he knew the standard which he was transgressing. And although the terms 'golden Latin' and 'the silver age' were not coined until the next century, the ideas and assumptions those terms were to express were a part of the humanist inheritance entrenched in Dryden's mind and imagination.

I come now to illustration and demonstration, and am aware in what follows that rather a lot is made to depend on a very little, but I hope that the little points will be sufficient to suggest the cogency of the larger argument. I intend to draw attention to aspects of Dryden's artistry by way of comparison with Denham in their versions of the death of Priam (narrated at *Æneid* II, 506–58). Dryden himself almost invites this comparison, for he concluded the episode with a direct borrowing of a whole line from Denham which he acknowledged in a note.[5]

It should be said at the outset that Denham's translation of much of Book II of the *Æneid* published under the title *The Destruction of Troy* in 1656 is a version of quality. This is particularly obvious when contrasted with his immediate predecessors, Phaer and Twyne (1558–84), Vicars (1632), and Ogilby (1647). He has poetic talent, and translates Virgil effectively into a modern idiom. He is a pioneer in the new mode of translation that leads in a direct line to Dryden and Pope. It is only when put alongside Dryden that Denham's artistry might seem rudimentary and deficient.

I start with a very little point about the opening line of the episode in the two translations:

> Now *Priams* fate perhaps you may enquire
> (*Destruction of Troy*, 496)

> Perhaps you may of *Priam*'s Fate enquire.
> (II, 691)[6]

Dryden's change of word order and emphasis brings with it a more even accentuation, giving the line in Dryden both more lilt and a more regular underlying beat. There is throughout a greater metrical certainty and assurance in Dryden; but Dryden's claim was for sweetness of sound and metrical harmony.

The prevailing sweetness of sound is most clearly demonstrated where perhaps it might be least expected, in the brutal climax of Priam's death. If we compare the two translations, it is apparent that the underlying harmony is not such as to detract from the impact of what is being described; paradoxically the horror is intensified. Denham first:

> So through
> His Sons warm bloud, the trembling King he drew
> To th' Altar; in his hair one hand he wreaths;
> His sword, the other in his bosom sheaths.
>
> (538–41)

Now Dryden:

> With that he dragg'd the trembling Sire,
> Slidd'ring through clotter'd Blood, and holy Mire,
> (The mingl'd Paste his murder'd Son had made,)
> Haul'd from beneath the violated Shade;
> And on the Sacred Pile, the Royal Victim laid.
> His right Hand held his bloody Fauchion bare;
> His left he twisted in his hoary Hair:
> Then, with a speeding Thrust, his Heart he found:
> The lukewarm Blood came rushing through the wound,
> And sanguine Streams distain'd the sacred Ground.
>
> (II, 748–57)

What is less than four lines in Denham has been expanded to fully ten lines, including two triplets, in Dryden, with much more specific and repellent physical detail; but the dignified rhythm, marked here by subtle effects of alliteration and assonance ('The mingl'd Paste his murder'd Son had made'), as in Homer and Virgil, sustains the elevated tone even in the least elevated moments of the epic, and honours Priam, the Royal Victim, in the gross indignity of his death, with a kind of poetic dignity. There is pathos but also dignity as the lukewarm blood is transmuted into the generalized formula of the 'sanguine Streams' (757) at the end.

'Yet his numbers are perpetually varied to increase the delight of his reader', Dryden said of Virgil. There is also greater metrical variety in Dryden than Denham. My example here is the pursuit of Polites by Pyrrhus. First Denham:

> Mean while *Polites* one of *Priams* sons
> Flying the rage of bloudy *Pyrrhus*, runs
> Through foes & swords, & ranges all the Court
> And empty Galleries, amaz'd and hurt,
> *Pyrrhus* pursues him, now oretakes, now kills,
> And his last blood in *Priams* presence spills.
>
> (518–23)

Now Dryden:

> Behold *Polites*, one of *Priam*'s Sons,
> Pursu'd by *Pyrrhus*, there for safety runs.
> Thro Swords, and Foes, amaz'd and hurt, he flies
> Through empty Courts, and open Galleries:
> Him *Pyrrhus*, urging with his Lance, pursues;
> And often reaches, and his thrusts renews.
> The Youth transfix'd, with lamentable Cries
> Expires, before his wretched Parent's Eyes:
>
> (II, 718–25)

Denham is impressive, and leads the way. Dryden has taken from him
several doublets: 'Through foes & swords' (520), 'amaz'd and hurt'
(521), 'the Court and empty galleries' (520–1), and rearranged them,
again allowing himself more scope by turning Denham's six lines into
eight. One little refinement on Denham is Dryden's well-vowelled line
'Through empty Courts, and open Galleries' (721). Is it fanciful to hear
in the collocation of like but slightly varied sounds an echoing effect that
suggests the distance covered in this ghastly chase? But my main point
in this example is about metrical variety. It is not simply a question of
Dryden having greater variety in his distribution of pauses. The danger,
intricacy, and length of the pursuit are heightened in Dryden by a
greater suppleness in the syntax. Denham's syntax is simple and
straightforward. In one long sentence, while Polites runs, Pyrrhus
pursues him, overtakes him, and kills him in Priam's presence; the sense
is extended over six lines. In Dryden, the sense is contained in each
couplet. The focus moves from Polites to Pyrrhus, back to Polites, and
on to Priam. The phrase 'Pursu'd by *Pyrrhus*' (719) interrupts his run for
safety. In the next line the subject is delayed until the final foot, 'he flies'
(720). The first line of the ensuing couplet is Latinate in its word order;
there is a suspension of the sense with the object coming before the
subject, and an interrupting clause before the main verb at the end,
'pursues' (722), so that the reader is propelled forward with Polites.
Although Polites is the object, the word order gives him primacy and
links him to the previous couplet. There is a similar effect in the
following line, 'Whom, gasping at his feet, when Priam saw' (726).
Poetical syntax gives variation, suspension, forward movement, and
backward connection.

Now for ornament of words. The example I want to focus on is the
description of the altar and the tree. First Denham:

> There stood an Altar open to the view
> Of Heaven, near which an aged Lawrel grew,
> Whose shady arms the houshold Gods embrac'd;
>
> (502–4)

Now Dryden:

> Uncover'd but by Heav'n, there stood in view
> An Altar; near the hearth a Lawrel grew;
> Dodder'd with Age, whose Boughs encompass round
> The Household Gods, and shade the holy Ground.
>
> (II, 700–3)

Three lines in Denham become four lines in Dryden, who brings out the figurative significance of the word 'ara' in the Latin[7] (the word is repeated in Virgil because, of course, the killing of Priam on the altar has sacrificial effect) by translating it as 'hearth' on its second appearance. In Latin, the word *ara* has warm associations apparent in the well-known formula 'pro aris et focis pugnare', 'to fight for altars and fires, for one's dearest possessions' (as translated in Lewis and Short). In English, 'altar' is a cold word, but 'hearth' is certainly warm, carrying the figurative associations of hearth and home.

The laurel is in the Latin 'veterrima' (513), 'very old'. Denham's 'aged' (503) becomes, in an inspired touch on the part of Dryden, 'Dodder'd' (702), which has both literal and figurative significance at the same time. The literal meaning as given in *OED* is 'Having lost the top or branches through age or decay', but Dryden uses 'doddered' to link with the doddery Priam's age, an imaginative licence derived from Virgil's description of Priam 'trementibus aevo … umeris' (509–10), 'with shoulders trembling with age'. But any indignity in the feebleness implied in 'doddered' is immediately countered by the beautifully dignified description of the tree's boughs in a line-and-a-half that has all the musicality of a Keats or Tennyson: 'encompass' (702) is a dignified, elegant, and sounding word. Here are Dryden's 'well-vowelled words', used not gratuitously but for a purpose, to evoke the sacred dignity of the setting, a dignity that is about to be sacrilegiously violated. Not all Dryden's words are chosen for their elegance, however. When Hecuba and the Trojan women take refuge at the altar, Dryden translates the Latin 'amplexae', 'embrace' (517), by the vernacular 'hug': 'Their images they hugg' (707), which captures better than the more formal 'embrace' their emotional desperation. Dryden's dignified style, largely the effect of word order and rhythm, does not exclude what Gerard Manley

Hopkins called 'the native thew and sinew of the English language'.[8] In fact, elegance is not the main criterion in Dryden's choice of words. 'Dodder'd', 'slidd'ring', 'clotter'd' – these are not elegant words, though they are sounding ones. The decorum of sound (where sound echoes sense) takes precedence over mere elegance. Though it would be dangerous to generalize about the diction of such a long work from such a short extract, it is worth noting that generalized formulaic diction like the 'sanguine streams' is little in evidence here. Verbal ornament is provided by sound and by the use of words that have both a literal and a figurative significance, the notable example here being 'dodder'd'.

It is also worth noting that the desire for what Dryden calls in his shorthand 'ornament of words' does not result in any impropriety of thought and expression. The same cannot always be said for Denham. When Denham's Pyrrhus is about to kill Priam 'in his hair one hand he wreathes; / His sword, the other in his bosom sheaths' (540–1). The ornament of words is improper here: while 'wreathe' might be an appropriate word to use in the context of two lovers, it is not so in this context, where Pyrrhus is gripping Priam's hair to get a firm purchase upon his body so that he can deliver what in Dryden is 'a speeding Thrust' (755). Dryden's line 'His left he twisted in his hoary hair' (754) properly relates words to things. To 'sheathe' the sword in his bosom, less improper than the use of 'wreathe', is also an elegantly indirect expression for a death-blow. Actions in Dryden are very directly represented. Perhaps 'hoary hair' might be regarded as a formula, but if so it is not one that in any way detracts from the immediacy of the action. Whether the weakness in Denham here is put down to the constraint of rhyme or to a misplaced pursuit of elegance, there can be no doubt about the superiority of Dryden's judgement and artistry.

Finally we come to the figures. Restraint in their use is enjoined by the Virgilian model. 'He is everywhere above the conceits of epigrammatic wit and gross hyperboles.' A notable hyperbole in Dryden occurs early on when he is describing the arming of Priam:

> His feeble shoulders scarce the weight sustain: ⎫
> Loaded, not arm'd, he creeps along, with pain; ⎬
> Despairing of Success; ambitious to be slain! ⎭
>
> (II, 697–9)

This triplet culminates in an Alexandrine that seems to have been worked up from the hint provided by Denham's 'not for their Fate, but to provoke his own' (501), taking the future participle *moriturus* (511) as meaning not merely 'doomed to die' but also expressing motive, 'with the intention to die'. It is certainly not an unmeaning or needless Alexandrine, though perhaps we would not miss it if it had not been there. The triplet as a whole emphasizes Priam's feebleness and the futility of his attempt, and brings out the human plight of the Trojan king. In his heroic plays and sometimes in his panegyrics, Dryden produced hyperboles that are indubitably gross. Here, Virgilian restraint is sacrificed a little in the interests of physical and emotional emphasis. Later the feebleness of Priam is again emphasized in hyperbolic language when the javelin that he throws 'seem'd to loiter as it flew' (743) before faintly tinkling on the shield. Dryden allowed his imagination to draw out pictorially what may only be implied in the Latin.

To sum up, what Dryden has done in a variety of ways (involving metrical refinement, the use of poetical syntax, attention to diction and sound, and deployment of the figures) is to add the ornaments of poetry to the comparatively bald substructure of Denham; in a word, he has endowed him with *ornatus*, ornament of language. Virgil was particularly associated with this term in the Renaissance, and his poetic style, in the comparison that was often made with the simpler style of Homer, was frequently distinguished from the Greek by virtue of its greater ornamentation. *Ornatus* is also the collective noun used by Cicero to embrace all the figures of rhetoric, whether figures of sense, of arrangement, or of sound, by which language is made forceful and emphatic. In all ancient rhetorical theory, and therefore in all literary and poetic theory in the Renaissance that has its starting-point in the rhetorical tradition, the ornamentation comprised of these figures is never an end in itself, but always a means to the greater end of clear and emphatic expressiveness. This is the justification for what Dryden calls his greater 'ornament of words'. What he has made clearer and more emphatic than Denham is the feebleness of old Priam, the sense of violation that his death over the altar entails, and the ugly horror of it all.

Yet there is a paradox here. As the last example relating to the use of the figures might suggest, in endowing his Virgil with the ornaments of art, even though it can be argued that his very idea and ideal of artistic excellence is derived from the example and authority of the Virgilian model, Dryden has changed what he has described as Virgil's poetical character in the process. As often, he is his own best commentator:

> Virgil therefore being so very sparing of his words, and leaving so much to be imagined by the reader, can never be translated as he ought in any modern tongue. To make him copious is to alter his character, and to translate him line for line is impossible ... Virgil

is much the closest of any Roman poet, and the Latin hexameter
has more feet than the English heroic.

(Preface to *Sylvae, Poems,* II, 243)

But having before observ'd, that *Virgil* endeavours to be short, and
at the same time Elegant, I pursue the Excellence, and forsake the
Brevity.

(*Dedication of the Æneis, Works,* V, 330)

Lay by *Virgil,* I beseech your Lordship, and all my better sort of
Judges, when you take up my Version, and it will appear a passable
Beauty, when the Original Muse is absent: But like *Spencer*'s false
Florimel made of Snow, it melts and vanishes, when the true one
comes in sight.

(*Dedication of the Æneis, Works,* V, 335)

But it may be that the Florimel effect is perhaps a general phenomenon
of all translation, however good; or at any rate translation of classic
originals. Look up almost any favourite passage from Virgil in Dryden's
version, and the first reaction will usually be one of disappointment. In
fairness, though, it must also be said that the Florimel effect can equally
work in reverse. It is quite possible to go from a particularly energetic
effect achieved by Dryden back to the original only to find something
that appears merely routine.

However that may be, the Virgilian standard, even when he deviated
from it, was a major factor informing Dryden's poetic practice. Neither
did artistic refinement come by accident, and nor was it inevitable: it
came by conscious design and application. In the *Ars poetica* (412–15),
Horace likens the poet's task and preparation to that of the Olympic
competitor or the musician who sings in honour of Apollo at the Pythian
games; all need to have at their disposal a mastery of technique that can
only be acquired by rigorous practice, so that it is then ready to be
harnessed for the great occasion. Dryden put his classical education to
good use and effected a *translatio studii* from Latin into English, to the
great benefit of his native tongue.

That Dryden brought a new refinement to English poetry is, of
course, an old truth, even if it is not always associated with his conscious
desire to emulate the achievements of the Augustan Latin classics. In his
'Life of Dryden', Dr Johnson alludes obliquely to this Roman connection
when he remarks 'What was said of Rome, adorned by Augustus, may be
applied by an easy metaphor to English poetry embellished by Dryden,
lateritiam invenit, marmoream reliquit, he found it brick and he left it

marble' (*Lives*, I, 469). More specifically, Johnson remarked that Dryden's name is venerated by every cultivator of English literature 'as he refined the language, improved the sentiments, and tuned the numbers of English poetry' (*Lives*, I, 419). This achievement is worthy of recall on the occasion of his tercentenary, because it is one for which, despite Johnson's praise, he has not always been given full credit.

There are perhaps two interrelated reasons for this. Appropriating Horace in his *Epistle to Augustus*, Pope pays Dryden a famous tribute, but in such a way as to reserve final perfection for his own age:

> Wit grew polite, and Numbers learn'd to flow.
> Waller was smooth; but Dryden taught to join ⎫
> The varying verse, the full resounding line, ⎬
> The long majestic march, and energy divine. ⎭
> Tho' still some traces of our rustic vein
> And splay-foot verse, remain'd, and will remain.
> Late, very late, correctness grew our care,
> When the tir'd nation breathed from civil war. ...
> Ev'n copious Dryden, wanted, or forgot,
> The last and greatest Art, the Art to blot.[9]

The Twickenham editors quote Pope's words to Spence: 'I learned versification wholly from Dryden's works; who had improved it much beyond any of our former poets; and would, probably, have brought it to its perfection, had not he been unhappily obliged to write so often in haste.' Dryden himself in a letter to Tonson in 1695 confessed: 'It wou'd require seaven yeares to translate Virgil exactly.'[10] In the Postscript to his *Æneis*, as already quoted, he admits to imperfection 'for want of Health and leisure to Correct it'. Is this disarming false modesty, or genuine self-criticism? Dryden's reputation as a hasty and sometimes negligent writer, forever fixed by the judgement of Pope, and Pope's own implicit claim to preside over the Augustan moment, have perhaps diverted attention somewhat from the purely artistic side of Dryden's achievement. Pope certainly brought his own well-known refinements to the couplet tradition, but the differences between himself and Dryden are surely differences between poets essentially equal in the reach of their art. Dryden and Pope, as our English Augustans, are justifiably paired, like their Roman artistic models and mentors, Virgil and Horace.

NOTES

1. This is printed in *Poems*, I, 11–12.
2. 'The Ovidian Elegiac Metre Described and Exemplified' in *Coleridge: Poetical Works*, edited by Ernest Hartley Coleridge (Oxford, 1969), p. 308.
3. See *The Poems of John Milton*, edited by John Carey and Alastair Fowler (London, 1968) pp. 456–7.
4. 'To the Earl of Roscommon on his Excellent *Essay on Translated Verse*' (1684), 11–23; *Poems*, II, 219.
5. 'A headless Carcass, and a nameless thing' (*Æneis*, II, 763); Dryden's note reads: '*This whole line is taken from Sir* John Denham' (*Works*, V, 405).
6. Quotations from Denham's translation and preface are taken from *The Poetical Works of Sir John Denham*, edited by Theodore Howard Banks, second edition (Hamden, CT, 1969) pp. 159–78. Dryden's translation is quoted from *Works*, V.
7. *Æneid* II, 513. The seventeenth-century vulgate text of Virgil does not differ substantially from modern ones in any of the passages under consideration here.
8. In a letter to Robert Bridges, 6 November 1887; see *Gerard Manley Hopkins: Selected Letters*, edited by Catherine Phillips (Oxford, 1990), p. 265.
9. Lines 267–73, 280–1; quoted from *The Twickenham Edition of the Poems of Alexander Pope*, Vol. IV: *Imitations of Horace*, edited by John Butt (London, 1939), pp. 217–18. The following prose quotation is from p. 218.
10. *The Letters of John Dryden*, edited by Charles E. Ward (Durham, N.C., 1942) p. 80.

Dryden: Classical or Neoclassical?

Kenneth Haynes

Dryden has been faulted for both defective and excessive decorum. Indecorous writing bothered nineteenth-century critics, such as Macaulay, especially; he loathed the 'filth' Dryden interpolated into his translation from Virgil. Twentieth-century readers in general have worried less about a lack of decorum in Dryden (though perhaps still worrying about prurience in *Sigismonda and Guiscardo*, as Wordsworth, for example, had done), or they have valued the way that Dryden moves among levels of diction and prized *Absalom and Achitophel* particularly.[1] Excessive decorum, on the other hand, has worried twentieth-century critics, particularly those not influenced by T. S. Eliot. Though Housman loved Dryden's ability to write a 'pure, wholesome, racy English' on occasion, he thought that Dryden's insistence on correctness and splendour mostly led him to ruin his poems. Pound, taking *nomen* as *omen*, found aridity to be the chief characteristic of Dryden. And in a discussion of Gavin Douglas's translation of Virgil, C. S. Lewis offers a scathing critique of the false classicism of Dryden's translation. The burden of this paper will be to answer Lewis and to think through the examples from Dryden which he contemns.[2]

Probably Ezra Pound's enthusiasm was responsible for the new appreciation of Douglas in the first part of the twentieth century. Pound wrote, notoriously, that Douglas's translation is 'better than the original', and even when on another occasion he stopped to say why, he added only that Douglas was better than Virgil at descriptions of the sea.[3] Still, by mid-century both Lewis and E. M. W. Tillyard could take Douglas's importance for granted.[4] Lewis does not invidiously contrast Virgil with Douglas's translation of Virgil as Pound did; instead, he invidiously contrasts Douglas's translation with Dryden's. His critical triangulation of Virgil, Douglas, and Dryden is roughly analogous to Keats's triangulation of Homer, Chapman, and Pope in the famous sonnet: both seek evidence in the earlier translation of an ancient writer's greatness and freshness that had become obscured by the later, overly classicizing translation. Lewis lists qualities in Douglas's translation that may strike us, he says, as very un-Virgilian: a certain cheerful briskness; admirable vividness; a delighted vision of Æneas' masculine beauty; and sensuous vitality in general. He then argues that this perception of Douglas as un-Virgilian is the result of our false picture of Virgil. Lewis writes:

> As soon as we become aware [of the real affinity between the ancient and the medieval world] we realize what it is that has made so many things in Douglas seem to us strangely un-Virgilian. It is not the real Virgil; it is that fatal 'classical' misconception of all ancient poets which the humanists have fastened upon our education – the spectral solemnity, the gradus epithets, the dictionary language, the decorum which avoids every contact with the senses and the soil ... Time after time Douglas is nearer to the original than any version could be which kept within the limits of later classicism. And that is almost another way of saying that the real Virgil is very much less 'classical' than we had supposed. To read the Latin again with Douglas's version fresh in our minds is like seeing a favourite picture after it has been cleaned. Half the 'richness' and 'sobriety' which we had been taught to admire turns out to have been only dirt; the 'brown trees' disappear and where the sponge has passed the glowing reds, the purples, and the transparent blues leap into life.
>
> (Lewis, p. 84)

Lewis makes his case by offering two examples of the contrast between Douglas and Dryden. The first is the description of Venus in the *Æneid*, I, 402: 'Rosea cervice refulsit'. Douglas gives 'her nek schane like unto the rois in May'. Dryden writes: 'she turn'd, and made appear / Her Neck refulgent'.[5] Lewis formulates two objections to Dryden's translation: first, he says, '*refulsit* cannot possibly have had for a Roman ear the "classical" quality which "refulgent" has for an English. It must have felt much more like "schane".' Second, he writes that '*rosea* has disappeared altogether in Dryden's version – and with it half the sensuous vitality of the image' (p. 84). A third objection could be added to Lewis's two: Dryden uses the adjective only in translations from Latin, never in his own poems or plays. In those instances, as here, it seems to serve as a kind of generalized marker announcing 'this is Latin', 'this is classical', rather than being vividly adjectival. This stands in contrast to Pope's usage of the word, which appears not only in his *Iliad* but also in the *Dunciad* and *The Rape of the Lock*; that is, it does not form part of a specialized vocabulary employed to create a closed classical world sealed off from the rest of experience.

However, a great deal is packed into Lewis's two objections that remains to be investigated; let us consider more slowly the nature of sensuous vitality in Virgil and what we mean by Latinate English in Dryden. How far should we be persuaded by Lewis's case for the real Virgil, whose verse delights in sensuous reality? After all, how sexy, how sensuous, is that shiny rosy neck? Or, for that matter, the ambrosial hair that follows in the next line? There is no answer, of course, since sex, like humour and dirt, so often prefers to stay at home and not be translated. Virgil certainly has had readers who have found his verse sensuous. Joseph Addison claimed that 'nothing can be ... more charming than [the figure] of Venus in the first Æneid'.[6] Montaigne insisted that Venus is even more beautiful in the *Æneid* than she is in reality, all naked and live and breathing. He was talking about the scene in Book VIII when she arouses Vulcan: 'niveis hinc atque hinc diva lacertis / cunctantem amplexu molli fovet'.[7] Modern readers may have difficulty believing that they and Montaigne are reading the same words.

Snowy arms, like the rosy neck and the ambrosial hair, may or may not be sexy; some readers, at least, will share Guy Davenport's exasperation at the 'blurred, depilated generalization' whenever bodies are described in the *Æneid*.[8] However, whatever our prejudices or tastes, let us steer clear of Lewis's implicit equation of sensuousness and the concrete. After all, the concrete and the specific can be just as conventional or just as unarousing as the abstract and the general. When Douglas in the prologue to his translation praises Virgil's works as 'lyke as the roys in June', for example, we are unlikely to find much there in the way of sensuous vitality. On the other hand, when Yeats refers (in 'A Woman Young and Old', VII) to his 'dark declivities', we may well feel that the abstract description is loaded with sexual import.

A second question raised by Lewis's first example concerns the nature of the Latin presence in Dryden's English. It is mistake to assume the presence of Latin in English poetry only occurs when a bit of Latin syntax appears, or a Latin-derived English word, or an array of polysyllables. Of course it may occur by those means. Milton favours the *ab urbe condita* construction ('after the Tuscan mariners transform'd', and the very title *Paradise Lost*); Dryden chooses 'refulgent' because of the etymological connection with 'refulsit'; and Shakespeare's great lines

> Will all great Neptune's ocean wash this blood
> Clean from my hand? No, this my hand will rather
> The multitudinous seas incarnadine,
> Making the green one red
>
> (*Macbeth* II.ii.60–3)

effectively oppose Latin polysyllables ('multitudinous', 'incarnadine') with English monosyllables ('green one red'). Great strength can be drawn from the presence of Latinate English, and of course so can obtuse obscurity.

However, the recreation of Roman weight and authority, of ancient magnificence, in English poetry is not necessarily obtained by these means, and does not necessarily rely on sesquipedalian sequences. Take Ben Jonson's praise of William Camden:

> What name, what skill, what faith hast thou in things!
> What sight in searching the most antique springs!
> What weight, and what authority in thy speech!
> Man scarce can make that doubt, but thou canst teach.[9]

These lines embody a Latin weight and authority but culminate in a line of monosyllables. There is a traditional understanding of monosyllables as exemplifying the 'Englishness' or 'Saxonnness' of the language. Jonson's line is perfectly English by that rough criterion, but it is also a direct translation of a sentence from Pliny ('nihil est quod discere velis quod ille docere non possit', *Epistles*, I, xxii). The frequently-renewed complaint about the wrenching of natural English to make it more Latin ignores how often the two are able to coexist without tension.

Even when inspired by Latin examples, splendour in English poetry is not usually attained by forcing English to conform to Latin. T. S. Eliot quoted Shakespeare's 'the kingdom of perpetual night' as an example of an English equivalent to the magnificence of Seneca's Latin at its best precisely because Seneca had been absorbed rather than imitated.[10] That is, the line is successful without having to invoke a linguistic ghost of *nox perpetua*; it recreates Latin magnificence in English without strain. Or take an example from *Paradise Lost*: 'So clomb this first grand Thief into Gods fold' (IV, 192). It is a portentous line, the *genus sublime dicendi* in action, but it does not include any polysyllable besides 'into'. Shortly following is a line entirely of monosyllables.

Dryden's strength in the *Æneid* is often of this kind. English and Latin power appear to be one:

> An Empire from its old Foundations rent,
> And ev'ry Woe the *Trojans* underwent:
> A Peopl'd City made a Desart Place;
> All that I saw, and part of which I was:
> (II, 5–8; *Works*, V, 379)

Perhaps in no other translation does Æneas sound like a great commander. His authority sounds in his words 'A peopl'd city made a Desart place / All that I saw and part of which I was', but they do not derive their force from Latin etymologies or syntax. Eric Griffiths, for example, has written perceptively about Dryden's effective contrasting of Saxon and Latin ways of writing English.[11] In these lines, however, which include a powerful monosyllabic line ('All that I saw, and part of which I was'), English and Latin are not contrasted but felt as one. Lewis's '*refulsit*'/'refulgent' example misrepresents the nature of Dryden's mastery in writing English with Latin power.

C. S. Lewis's second complaint centres on Dryden's refusal to translate certain words. In his *Dedication of the Æneis*, Dryden writes that he cannot translate *mollis amaracus* as 'sweet marjoram', since such 'Village-words' give the reader 'a mean Idea of the thing' (*Works*, V, 335). So Ascanius is laid down on a 'flow'ry bed' rather than on soft marjoram (I, 974). Douglas, unsurprisingly, has no qualms about 'tendir mariolyne', and Lewis feels that Douglas's adherence to the vernacular gives him a decisive advantage over Dryden.

The example from Dryden is famous, or infamous, but it is more peculiar than critics have realized. Certainly it is difficult for us to understand or have sympathy for Dryden here. We need only recall the uses of 'marjoram' in four works by Shakespeare: as the password in *King Lear*; in the beautiful list of flowers in the *Winter's Tale*; in Sonnet 99; and in *All's Well that Ends Well*. However, we should note that the rejection of 'marjoram' and the search for alternatives to it were long-lasting, not merely a prejudice of one man or one age. It is not surprising to find Christopher Pitt explaining in a note to his translation that (like Dryden) he could not write 'surrounded him with sweet marjoram' because it 'would not sound gracefully in English'.[12] However, it *is* surprising to learn that Wordsworth, too, avoids it in his translation from the first Book of the *Æneid*, preferring 'amaracus'. No-one would accuse Tennyson of being ashamed of village flowers, but he too prefers 'amaracus' to 'marjoram', in these lines from *Oenone*:

> And at their feet the crocus brake like fire,
> Violets, amaracus, and asphodel,
> Lotos and lilies[13]

Between Robert Herrick and John Clare, I have found only one example of 'marjoram' in a major poet: Christopher Smart, in *Jubilate Agno*: 'Let Athlai rejoice with Bastard Marjoram.'

To get a better purchase on the example, take a more accessible instance, from Pope's *Iliad*, where Pope justifies his refusal to translate the word 'ass' on the grounds that 'upon the whole, a Translator owes so much to the Taste of the Age in which he lives, as not to make too great a Complement to the former'.[14] We might naturally have sympathy with Pope here (as we do not naturally have sympathy with his expunging the word 'hats' from Shakespeare's *Julius Caesar*, II.i). An ass in Pope's day (as in ours) was not (as in Homer's time) a good comparison for the unwillingness to retreat, since it is so often associated with 'clumsiness, ignorance, stupidity' (*OED*). In addition, there is the uncomfortable phonetic proximity to 'arse', which worried the eighteenth century and which ultimately resulted in the obscure creation of 'donkey' in 1785. However, in the case of 'marjoram', there is no awkward homophony or changed meaning; it is very hard to hear what the associations must have been.

Perhaps the most famous, and an even more perplexing, instance in English is Johnson's discussion of Lady Macbeth's speech including that line of great dramatic power, 'That my keen knife see not the wound it makes', incidentally another line exclusively of monosyllables. Johnson writes that 'all the force of poetry' is exerted in this passage; nonetheless, he is disturbed by the disparity between the words and the ideas. The sentiment 'is weakened by the name of an instrument used by butchers and cooks in the meanest employment; we do not immediately conceive that any crime of importance is to be committed with a *knife*'.[15] This is Johnson, recall, the man who magisterially dismisses Dennis's neoclassical scruples about Shakespeare having represented a senator in *Coriolanus* as a buffoon: 'wanting a buffoon, he went into the senate-house for that which the senate-house would certainly have afforded him'.[16]

However, before we assent to this picture of ancient and medieval common sense and sensuous vitality as against a subsequent etiolated classicizing that infected even the robust good sense of Johnson, let us raise two questions. First, how free is Virgil himself from taboos against low words? Second, how well does the example represent Dryden's usual practice?

In the Nisus and Euryalus episode in Book IX, Euryalus kills Rhamnes who is asleep, snoring in a drunken stupor. Virgil, however, avoids the verb 'to snore' (*sterto* in Latin), a verb that was good enough for Lucretius and would be good enough for Milton, as the Greek was good enough for Aeschylus. Instead, he writes that Rhamnes 'blew forth sleep from his whole breast' ('toto proflabat pectore somnum'). Servius compliments Virgil on the periphrasis which enables him to avoid the low word *sterto*. Dryden, in contrast, has no problem with 'snore'. He preserves it in translations of Lucretius, Homer, Juvenal, and Persius, and he introduces it into this very episode of the *Æneid*. Nisus and Euryalus, he writes:

> found the careless Hoast dispers'd upon the Plain:
> Who gorg'd, and drunk with Wine, supinely snore
>   (IX, 423–4; *Works*, VI, 653)

Note that Dryden even uses 'snore' as a rhyme word. In Charles Cotton's burlesque of the *Æneid* (1664, 1665), which opens

> I sing the man, (read it who list,
> A Trojan true as ever pist)

several rhymes on 'snore' are offered as ludicrous deflation. So the danger of a lack of decorum was certainly present, as it was with Virgil. However, Dryden, unlike Virgil, is unembarrassed before a simple function of the body. We should view Dryden in this instance in a light opposite from that in which Lewis places him. Dryden in this passage has more contact with the senses and the body than Virgil does, and his unwillingness to translate 'marjoram' is simply not the same as 'the decorum which avoids every contact with the senses and the soil'.

However, to have discussed the matter in this way is still not to challenge a powerful literary prejudice. Periphrasis, abstraction, generalization, the elements of the high style, do not have to imply the absence of contact with the senses and the soil; this is Lewis's unexamined premise. The high style does insist on a heightened seriousness, and this may manifest itself in formality. It makes sense for Machiavelli to have dressed in his finest before reading the classics. Such formality may exclude humour and the life of the body; anthropologists point to control over the body and anxiety over humour as good markers of the formality of a social scene. All too easily, this may become the impoverished formality which Lewis sees in Dryden's translation, and which, we should perhaps admit, is occasionally a defect in Virgil's *Æneid*. However, the high style does not have to take this form. It can include without embarrassment or tension contact with the senses and the soil. Homer doesn't worry about snoring or about whether princesses should be playing ball games; Alexandrian critics do. Or high and low elements may coexist within it comprehensively but variously and variably in tension, transfiguring each other or failing to do so, as so often in Shakespeare.

One way to understand the high style is to see it as possessing a 'utopian function'. The phrase is portentous and seems to invoke Ernst Bloch. However, it also occurs helpfully in Paul Ricoeur's *Lectures on Ideology and Utopia* (a work that draws on Karl Mannheim's *Ideology and Utopia*). Two points from Ricoeur's work are relevant here: first, that the engagement of utopian thought with reality can be astonishingly diverse; and second, that from the no-place of ou-topia one has, in general, the choice to face the world or to turn one's back to it.

Before considering the high style in this light, let us first examine the well-known example of literary panegyric. The utopian cast of formal praise might certainly be mere flattery, mere ideology, a result of ignoring the circumstances of the world; or it might be hortatory, offering a vision of an order that ought to be actually present; or indeed, if the discrepancy between the praise and the reality is great enough, it may be subversive. Unsurprisingly, this elementary taxonomy is too crude to account for the power of most fine poetry, though perhaps it is a useful start. How should we understand these lines from Dryden's *Threnodia Augustalis?*

> But ere a Prince is to Perfection brought,
> He costs omnipotence a second thought.
> (437–8; *Poems*, II, 416)

Are we actually to imagine God the Father scratching his head and muttering to himself 'Now here's a tough one'? The audience presumably relished the sublime absurdity of the lines. The tone is everything here, controlling through wittily acknowledged exaggeration what might otherwise be ideology. It is successful because we are unable to say, exactly, what is absurd. Not the prince, the poet, the divine, but somehow the whole assemblage, which does not, however, thereby lose its significance.

The high style has a similar range of utopian implications. It might be an evasion or elision of reality, the loss of sensuous contact, the purging of marjorams from the world, which Lewis dreads. It might be the placing of everyday reality within an intellectual order. So in Dryden's *Georgics* we have the 'bearded product' for corn and both 'scaly flocks' and 'scaly nations' for fish. Perhaps we should understand these periphrases as statements about the pre-Linnaean order of nature, as Donald Davie once suggested, though to my mind unpersuasively.[17]

Or the high style might be a transfiguring of the quotidian, a vision of the ordinary redeemed of the accidental. Pater wrote that Leonardo's teacher Verrocchio was the 'designer ... of all things for sacred or household use ... making them fair to look upon, filling the common ways of life with the reflexion of some far-off brightness'.[18] This is something we may also experience in great poetry, the common ways of life filled with a far-off brightness. Dryden's ambition in his translation of the *Æneid* was to be 'Grave, Majestical, and Sublime';[19] to see this, with Lewis, as necessarily spectral, sterile, and dictionary-bound is as mistaken as to be coerced by it.

Since Lewis was contrasting Douglas's translation with Dryden's, he had no opportunity to consider Dryden's version of the *Georgics*. It would have been extremely strange to accuse Dryden of an excess of decorum in that work. Recall, for example, Macaulay's objection: Dryden 'polluted the sweet and limpid poetry of the *Georgics* with filth which would have moved the loathing of Virgil'. The world of the *Georgics* is different from that of the *Æneid*, both in Virgil and in Dryden, in part because the genre does not require as great an elevation of diction as the epic. Let us look at one bit of interpolated filth, the description in Book III concerning the stallion now in its old age:

> But worn with Years, when dire Diseases come,
> Then hide his not Ignoble Age, at Home:
> In Peace t' enjoy his former Palms and Pains;
> And gratefully be kind to his Remains.
> For when his Blood no Youthful Spirits move,
> He languishes and labours in his Love.
> And when the sprightly Seed shou'd swiftly come,
> Dribling he drudges, and defrauds the Womb.
>
> (151–8; *Works*, V, 213)

Dryden is infinitely more explicit and detailed than Virgil, and he stresses in the heavy alliteration the gross physical details. The question is no longer one of the neoclassical, of false elevation, but of whether classical decorum can sustain the weight of such indecorous details. I think it does; one of the things to value in Dryden is his ability to move from tragedy to farce and back, to leave us unsure whether we are experiencing tragedy or farce. His ranging across tones and levels of diction often enables him to catch or recreate the complex interplay of voices in Virgil.

It would not be useful to generalize about the neoclassical in Dryden ('neoclassical' understood here not historically but critically, distinguishing a sclerotic from a true classical style), since his practice differs among and even within his works. Because of its insistence on a sustained decorum, *All for Love*, for example, forfeits the powerful effects

Shakespeare gains by placing colloquial words in a high context; there is
no equivalent to 'By Isis I will give thee bloody teeth', or 'I saw her once
hop forty paces through the public street', or 'a lass unparalleld' in *All
for Love*. Relative to Virgil, Dryden's translation of the *Æneid* moves
both closer to (in the case of 'snore') and further from (in the case of
'marjoram') the circumstances of the world. In the *Georgics*, and
elsewhere, we have a utopian vision of an ideal order, but we also have
the cost of the order, unceasing labour; and we also have mud between
our toes; in the phrase from *Threnodia*, we have 'paradise manured' (363;
Poems, II, 411).

NOTES

1. Macaulay, *The History of England: from the Accession of James the Second*,
   edited by C. H. Firth, 6 vols (London, 1915), II, 852, quoted in David
   Hopkins, *John Dryden* (Cambridge, 1986), p. 127; Wordsworth, *The Critical
   Opinions of William Wordsworth* (Baltimore, 1950), pp. 246–7.
2. Housman, 'The Name and Nature of Poetry', in *Collected Poems and Selected
   Prose of A. E. Housman*, edited by Christopher Ricks (Harmondsworth,
   1988), pp. 349–71 (p. 359); Lewis, *English Literature in the Sixteenth Century
   Excluding Drama* (Oxford, 1954; hereafter 'Lewis'), pp. 83–4.
3. Pound, 'Mr Housman at Little Bethel', *Literary Essays of Ezra Pound*, edited
   by T. S. Eliot (London, 1954), pp. 66–73 (p. 70); 'How to Read', *Literary
   Essays*, pp. 15–50 (p. 35).
4. Tillyard, *The English Epic and its Background* (New York, 1954).
5. Dryden's I, 556–7; *Works*, I, 361.
6. Addison, *Spectator*, 28 June 1712.
7. *Æneid*, VIII, 387–8; Montaigne, 'Sur des vers de Virgile', *Essais*, III, 5.
8. Guy Davenport, 'On Some Lines of Virgil', *Eclogues* (San Francisco, 1981).
9. 'To William Camden', 7–10; *Ben Jonson: Poems*, edited by Ian Donaldson
   (London, 1975), p. 13.
10. *Richard III*, I.iv.48; T. S. Eliot, 'Seneca in Elizabethan Translation', in
    Eliot, *Selected Essays* (London, 1976), pp. 65–105 (p. 90).
11. Eric Griffiths, 'Dryden's Past', *PBA*, 84 (1994), 113–49.
12. Pitt's note on his I, 934; *The Works of Virgil in Latin and English*, 4 vols
    (London, 1778), II, 120.
13. Lines 94–6; *The Poems of Tennyson*, edited by Christopher Ricks, second
    edition, 3 vols (Harlow, 1987), I, 426.
14. The *Twickenham Edition of the Poems of Alexander Pope*, VIII: *The Iliad of
    Homer, Books X–XXIV*, edited by Maynard Mack (London, 1967), p. 64
    (note to XI, 668).
15. *The Rambler*, 26 October 1751; quoted from *The Yale Edition of the Works of
    Samuel Johnson*, V: *The Rambler*, edited by W. J. Bate and Albrecht B.
    Strauss (New Haven, 1969), p. 127.
16. *Preface to Shakespeare*, in *The Yale Edition*, VII: *Johnson on Shakespeare*,
    edited by Arthur Sherbo (New Haven, 1968), p. 65.

17. Donald Davie, 'The Language of Science and the Language of Literature', *Older Masters* (New York, 1992), p. 84.

18. *The Works of Walter Pater*, 8 vols (London, 1900), I: *The Renaissance*, p. 101.

19. *Dedication of the Æneis*; *Works*, V, 267.

Dryden's Criticism as Transfusion

Philip Smallwood

It is now quite normal to join company with Dryden's contemporaries
and immediate successors and to view him as England's greatest
translator of the classical Roman poets (and a range of other material).
New work on Dryden's translations, and their literary contexts, pre-texts
and determinants, has substantially modified the image of Dryden as a
religious or satirical writer or the negotiator of such contemporary events
as the Popish Plot. Scholars have, to be sure, continued to detect topical
resonances in Dryden's poetry, increasingly within a variety of osten-
sibly non-political works: as Howard Erskine-Hill has written, 'The
pervasiveness of Jacobite and Williamite allusion in Dryden's *Aeneis* may
be readily traced.'[1] But Dryden scholars have also rediscovered the
literary context of their primary texts: the social and the political (the
'manners', in contemporary terminology) has transformed into the
mental and emotional world of the poet, and we now view Dryden in
company with his sources in a collaborative partnership, or spiritual
communion, of poetic souls.

Interest in the relationship between Dryden's literary critical writing
and its historical antecedents, the subject of the present discussion, has
lagged behind this important shift. Part of the problem may be that to
use the term 'literary criticism' of any of Dryden's writing is inevitably
to make certain assumptions about what criticism is.[2] In recent years
commentators have attempted to collapse criticism into 'cultural studies',
or to redefine it as 'theory',[3] and it is sometimes described as a hybrid
mode or 'bastard discourse' within the debates of philosophical writing.
Dryden himself defined it in his 'Author's Apology for Heroic Poetry
and Poetic Licence' simply as 'a standard of judging well' (*Essays*, I,
197). But to admit into the category of criticism Dryden's collected
essays, dialogues, prefaces, and epistles dedicatory in prose, or to include
the many occasions on which he is explicitly alluding to, translating,
adapting, and implicitly judging, placing, appreciating, or otherwise
interpreting other poets, or copying and re-stating other critics, would
be to invoke an inescapably controversial definition of the critical
process.[4] To this core problem of what actually counts as criticism in
Dryden, we must then add the difficulties of thinking historically about

it, given the historical models available to us with which to think. Our conception of Dryden would seem to be partial cause and partial consequence of our idea of history and our conception of criticism.

My suggestion in this paper is that recent critiques of romanticist historicism have disclosed a way of thinking afresh about the present critical value of Dryden. One tendency of attempts to restructure literary history by destabilizing the literary text has been to look within the consciousness of the reader for the meaning of its past. Correspondingly, the text of criticism, like the text of literature, or like the 'text' that is the postmodern past itself, is re-created in the context of reception by each new reading. At the same time, I suggest, this internalization (or mentalization) by the reader of the decomposed trace of the past brings our postmodern return to Dryden closer to the process of Dryden's own re-creation. Dryden re-created his source-texts through translation, and wrote, apropos of Chaucer, that 'nothing [is] lost out of nature, though every thing is altered' (*Essays*, II, 285). His work helps us to see historical thought in R. G. Collingwood's extended sense as an operation of 're-enactment'.[5] The pathos of this 'alteration' is known to everyone who has experienced the restlessness, rapidity and 'giddy turns' of recent critical 'revolution', where 'Nature knows / No stedfast Station, but, or Ebbs, or Flows'.[6] To revise the idea of history that we bring to the history of criticism might suggest how the critical past can enter into the present. More specifically, the new historical terms can alert us to the role Dryden played within the limits dictated by his own perspective, in an age of Rymer and rules, and then to the possible relevance of his criticism in the present. Criticism's past can be not only the source or cause of, but also a defamiliarizing alternative to, the critical present.

*   *   *

When Samuel Johnson wrote of Dryden as 'the father of English criticism', as 'the writer who first taught us to determine upon principles the merit of composition' (*Lives*, I, 410), he spelt out an idea of criticism that he shared with Dryden. It is one that we have not entirely abandoned. At the same time, the legacy of romantic historicism seems also to dictate that Dryden belongs only to criticism's primitive, unfinished life. His merits are superseded in the fact that they are relative entirely to their age, in the perception that John Dryden (the critic of the later seventeenth century who challenged neoclassical rules) is not Thomas Rymer (who did not). There could be no better illustration of this sense of the past as the confused means to the clearer, more complete, and more perfect end that is the critical present than Dryden's

showing in the latest histories of criticism. The recently-published fourth
volume of *The Cambridge History of Literary Criticism* can exemplify my
point.

To work through the references to Dryden's criticism in this
monument to modern historical practice is to see how far it has
successfully *dissolved* him. To the modern historian, Dryden's criticism
is not distinctive for any capacity to evoke or explain aesthetic or
emotional effects which we are unfamiliar with, or have ceased to feel.
Instead, Dryden's statements on matters of theory, notably the taxonomy
of genre and literary type, are felt to possess a convenient typicality.
Dryden expresses the period's 'topics and modes'.[7] His role, like those of
Batteux and Du Bos, for example, is that of the 'theorist of imitation' (p.
739). Dryden, according to an essay on 'Theories of Language', was
among critics who condemned 'word-play' and 'puns'. Such 'harmonious
nonsense' he saw as 'false Wit'. In common with the philosophy of
Locke, critics like Dryden 'typically reduced figurative language to the
status of mere "ornament"' (p. 337). And in the understanding of artistic
illusion, later critics like Lessing or Mendelssohn observed what
Dryden, from his earlier peg on the historical scale, had failed to spot:
'The notions of literary creation expressed by Gerard, Duff, and Young
are far removed from those of Hobbes and Dryden' (p. 631).

Dryden, by comparison, belongs with Pope. Both are conservatively
defined. Both 'press the ancient claim' (p. 14). Dryden had, indeed,
drawn on the past of criticism for contemporary purposes throughout his
life. To the French critics of his own generation who had made the texts
of classical literary criticism new for their time, Dryden gave particular
attention. Boileau and Rapin, he wrote in 'The Author's Apology for
Heroic Poetry', were 'the greatest of this age', the latter being 'alone
sufficient, were all other critics lost, to teach anew the rules of writing'
(*Essays*, I, 199). But when the historians elucidate Dryden's debt to the
critical past, they move between the compulsive regularizer who 'brings
his criticism into line with the French' (p. 178), the stumbling emulator
and crass modernizer who 'attempt[s] to imitate Boileau's neo-classical
appropriation of Longinus' (p. 396), or the critical lightweight who
found that a metaphor by Hobbes 'took [his] fancy' (p. 615). To use such
language is to make neo-romantic judgements about Dryden's historical
situation. In this description, Dryden's critical statements, being rooted
in the past, are simply no longer of interest to us: they lack pertinence.

Such judgements stand in sharp contrast to the understanding of
Dryden's historical position, seen within a shared idea of criticism,
possessed by Samuel Johnson. For example, to the Cambridge historians,
Dryden on Shakespeare resembles Ben Jonson on Shakespeare, and is

'comparatively sketchy' (p. 370). But Samuel Johnson viewed what Dryden had said of Shakespeare as the paternal seed of all later attempts at Shakespearean criticism, including his own. 'The account of Shakespeare', he writes of the *Essay of Dramatic Poesy*,

> may stand as a perpetual model of encomiastick criticism; exact without minuteness, and lofty without exaggeration. The praise lavished by Longinus, on the attestation of the heroes of Marathon by Demosthenes, fades away before it. In a few lines is exhibited a character, so extensive in its comprehension and so curious in its limitations, that nothing can be added, diminished, or reformed; nor can the editors and admirers of Shakespeare, in all their emulation of reverence, boast of much more than of having diffused and paraphrased this epitome of excellence, of having changed Dryden's gold for baser metal, of lower value though of greater bulk.
>
> (*Lives*, I, 412)

Johnson quoted the entire passage from Dryden – recently alluded to in Frank Kermode's new book on the language of Shakespeare – at the end of his 'Preface'.[8] Elements of its rhetorical organization are reflected in the 'Preface' itself, and in a remark that seems to encompass a debt both to the poetry and to criticism. In a comment of special importance to the contemporary currency of 'classical' literary criticism, Johnson pays tribute in the 'Life of Dryden' to 'the criticism of a poet; not a dull collection of theorems, nor a rude detection of faults ... but a gay and vigorous dissertation, where delight is mingled with instruction, and where the author proves his right of judgement by his power of performance' (*Lives*, I, 412).

For Johnson, it was by this 'power of performance' that Dryden had simultaneously transcended and transfused into his own practice the past of literary criticism. Two hundred and fifty years later in the *Cambridge History*, Dryden's importance both to the past and to the present of criticism is by comparison lost as a coherent historical 'event'. The reasons why Dryden might be a maker of history, one whose past shapes the context that shapes our present, few readers will guess. The warmth of Johnson's praise will seem incomprehensible.

The task of critical history at the present time, I therefore suggest, must be to reinstate Dryden, and to do so in terms that correspond with his 'power of performance'. Not all occasions where Dryden is echoing earlier critical statements qualify as 'transfusions' in the sense I wish to commend. Dryden did not baulk at absorbing sections from Segrais's

Preface to Virgil unchanged into his own long introduction. In George Watson's edition of Dryden's essays, these passages are omitted – judiciously, perhaps. On the other hand, as commentators have shown, Dryden is creatively adopting the figures and voices of other critics in the 'Discourse of Satire'.[9] And here, according to Watson's note, Dryden's 'handling of his scholarly sources ... is ... full of his own personality' (*Essays*, II, 97). Sometimes, Dryden's critical echoes are not of scholarly sources as such, but teasings or provocations of critics who are still breathing. In 'The Grounds of Criticism in Tragedy', Dryden mocks Shakespeare while he parodies the sarcastic critical style of Rymer:

> What a pudder is here kept in raising the expression of trifling thoughts! Would not a man have thought that the poet had been bound prentice to a wheelwright, for the first rant? and had followed a ragman for the clout and blanket, in the second.
>
> (*Essays*, I, 258)

Here, in language quite unlike his usual 'fragrance and flowers' (Johnson, *Lives*, I, 413), Dryden suggests the mutual sensitivity involved in his dialogue with Rymer. George Saintsbury's *History of Criticism* castigates Rymer as 'intensely stupid', and J. W. H. Atkins describes Rymer's critical efforts as, in contrast with Dryden's, 'almost wholly misleading'; *The Cambridge History* mentions Rymer only in passing, and curiously avoids a verdict on his work.[10] But Rymer and Dryden are working within sufficiently close channels to share a joke at Shakespeare's (and each other's) expense. Dryden's language recognizes a satirical wisdom in Rymer's deployment of 'classical' rules, and his Rymerese has this mutuality as its subtext. The complexity of Dryden's response to the living critic who responded to him, along with his ability to remake in his own terms – rather than simply observe or interpret – the dead past of criticism, demands some alternative sense of the historical 'event'.

My suggestion is that history requires an expansion in the 'modes of relation' conventionally permitted between the critical text and the contexts by which it is known. Paradoxically, the 'events' of criticism, of which Dryden's encomium on Shakespeare is one, are most fully conceived as history when they are most fully appreciated aesthetically. To arrange the past in narrative terms is a precondition of history writing. But if the reasons for change in the critical past are to be appreciated as plausible today, the reader of history needs to experience more of its moments as depths. I propose for special attention a passage from the Preface to the *Fables* in which Dryden is introducing the *Iliad*. Tone, language, and rhetorical organization, in addition to content, all contribute indistinguishably here to an 'event' received as criticism then, but expressive of standards which implicate or indict criticism now:

> And this I dare assure the world beforehand, that I have found, by trial, Homer a more pleasing task than Virgil ... For the Grecian is more according to my genius than the Latin poet. In the works of the two authors we may read their manners and natural inclinations, which are wholly different. Virgil was of a quiet, sedate temper: Homer was violent, impetuous, and full of fire. The chief talent of Virgil was propriety of thoughts, and ornament of words: Homer was rapid in his thoughts, and took all the liberties, both of numbers and of expressions, which his language, and the age in which he lived, allowed him. Homer's invention was more copious, Virgil's more confined ... our two great poets, being so different in their tempers, one choleric and sanguine, the other phlegmatic and melancholic; ... the action of Homer, being more full of vigour than that of Virgil, according to the temper of the writer, is of consequence more pleasing to the reader. One warms you by degrees; the other sets you on fire all at once, and never intermits his heat.
>
> (*Essays*, II, 274–6)

Behind Dryden's appreciation are Longinus (translated into French by Boileau in 1674), the various 'Comparaisons' between Greek and Roman authors composed by René Rapin, and the comparisons between Greek, Roman, Italian, Spanish, and modern French poetry by Dominique Bouhours.[11] But Dryden draws back in this passage from the detail of Homer's and Virgil's work, from the words and passages he had grappled with close-up as a translator, and invites us to consider cross-cultural categories that precede textuality – 'genius', 'inclinations', 'temper', and 'talent'. A conscious elevation of style combines medieval medical language (the 'choleric' and 'sanguine', the 'phlegmatic' and 'melancholic') with subdued alliterative touches – the 'full of fire', the 'copious' and 'confined', or the creative 'vigour' of Homer when compared with Virgil. This too is 'the criticism of a poet'. But as in Johnson's praise of Dryden's paragraph on Shakespeare, the comparison of Homer and Virgil is also 'lofty without exaggeration'. The visualizable gestures and conversational deferrals, the move from the polite aloofness of 'we' and 'the reader' to the familiar 'you' of the closing sentence, are closer to Montaigne than the dense metaphoric quality of Johnsonian prose, the 'thorns and brambles' of Rymer's (Johnson, *Lives*, I, 413), or the fussy magisterialism of Wordsworth's.

Dryden's comparison also integrates, in a single moment of self-
awakening and self-comprehension, the duality of his own vagrant poetic
personality. Hence it is not simply the result of applying any particular
'theory' of criticism, and cannot be explained by invoking a teleology of
ideas. What it does imply, as the background in Longinus, Rapin, and
Bouhours may suggest, is a structure of action, feeling, and thought that
belongs to tradition. Dryden's transitions in this passage from the
Preface to the *Fables* were recapitulated in Pope's 'Preface to the *Iliad*',
where Pope compares the habits and tempers of Virgil and Homer.[12]
They are later re-enacted in Johnson, using different but equally
comparable authors, and by reference to equally necessary and urgent,
but complex and intractable, criteria of judgement. In the 'Preface to
Shakespeare' of 1765, Johnson compares the 'easy, elevated and
harmonious' diction of Addison's *Cato* with that of Shakespeare's
Othello, 'the vigorous and vivacious offspring of observation impregnated
by genius', to find that while Addison speaks 'the language of poets',
Shakespeare's is that 'of men'.[13] Finally, and to come full circle, at the
close of his critical career in 1781, Johnson in the 'Life of Pope' weaves
elements drawn from Pope's and Dryden's 'essays' on Homer and Virgil
into his own 'parallel' (as he called it) of Dryden and Pope:[14]

> The style of Dryden is capricious and varied, that of Pope is
> cautious and uniform ... Dryden is sometimes vehement and rapid;
> Pope is always smooth, uniform, and gentle. Dryden's page is a
> natural field, rising into inequalities, and diversified by the varied
> exuberance of abundant vegetation; Pope's is a velvet lawn, shaven
> by the scythe, and levelled by the roller ... If the flights of Dryden
> are ... higher, Pope continues longer on the wing. If of Dryden's fire
> the blaze is brighter, of Pope's the heat is more regular and constant.
>
> (*Lives*, III, 222–3)

*   *   *

At the present time, when criticism as 'judgement' is overwhelmed by
other essentialist definitions, the model of Dryden's comparison of
Homer and Virgil – along with his judgements of Virgil, Lucretius,
Theocritus, and Horace in the Preface to *Sylvae*, of Juvenal, Persius, and
Horace in the *Discourse Concerning Satire*, and in the Preface to the
Fables of Boccaccio, Ovid, and Chaucer – can seem *merely* traditional, or
out of date. Such passages do not have the interest of 'theory', in the
precise regard that the nature of tragedy, satire, or epic is discussed at
other points in the essays. Neither are they 'practical criticism' in any

modern sense that commentators have tried, in vain to my mind, to argue.[15] Yet in a context of reception that questions distinctions of value, Dryden's judgements of classical and medieval writing can instance the different kind of critical history I am suggesting we need. Such a history creatively translates classical criticism into the present by giving a more plausible and interesting account of Dryden. It suggests the good things in criticism of the past that do not continue forever. But it also points to the perspective on the present of criticism that only the past can provide. The most desirable history thus maintains the ground for similarity and difference between critical present and past.

Dryden's is in more than one sense 'the criticism of a poet'. His poem on Milton, his satire on Shadwell in *Mac Flecknoe*, the moving memorial to Oldham, and the summary accounts of the literary-historical importance of Waller and Jonson in the verse translation of Boileau's *Art poétique*, have a double identity as verse-portraits of poets and as part of the corpus of his critical work. And the connections and contrasts Dryden expresses in the sequence of critical portraits of poets in his prefatory essays depend upon the same assumption of continuous standards across time that makes the poems of Virgil and Homer translatable. Such assumptions are the basis of the critical tradition that runs through Dryden. They point not towards assessments of a work's conformity to a species or genre, but towards pressing questions of preference and quality that transcend their place and time.

R. S. Crane argued as long ago as 1953 that historical treatment of the period 1650 to 1800 in criticism should

> exhibit critics speaking for themselves with respect to problems they themselves had formulated in the process of solving them, rather than problems set for them, after the event, by the historian ... Dryden and Johnson would still be the heroes of the story, but not because they helped to emancipate criticism from the tyranny of neoclassical rules ... [The history] could ... be expected to throw light not simply on the dead opinions and pronouncements of dead critics but on the permanent and still living problems of analysis and reasoning which critics in all times and traditions have faced, and concerning which we ourselves might easily profit, in a good many ways, by knowing in detail how they were defined and solved by our predecessors in the seventeenth and eighteenth centuries.[16]

In practice, however, historians seem by comparison too often to gaze on 'the dead opinions and pronouncements of dead critics'. Their thesis

precedes our aesthetic experience of the critics to which they refer. But
without a language to evoke the unsolved problems faced by criticism in
their own time, they are missing the 'self-knowledge of the mind'
without which, according to Collingwood, history proper cannot be
written.[17]

A thinker of more recent years who has also brought the idea of
history closer to the principles of classical translation as we find them in
Dryden is Hans-Georg Gadamer. According to Gadamer, 'The general
nature of tradition is such that only the part of the past that is not past
offers the possibility of historical knowledge.' In this view, romantic
historicism is replaced with a past and a present that enclose each other:
understanding a classic

> will always involve *more* than merely historically reconstructing the
> past 'world' to which the work belongs. Our understanding will
> always retain the consciousness that we too belong to that world,
> and correlatively, that the work too belongs to our world.
>
> This is just what the word 'classical' means: that the duration of
> a work's power to speak directly is fundamentally unlimited ...
> Cultural consciousness manifests an ultimate community and
> sharing with the world from which a classical work speaks.[18]

Thus defined, I am suggesting, the ideal of historical thinking about the
classics of literary criticism – for us as for Dryden – becomes comprehensible
as 'transfusion'. It is a 'sharing with the world from which a classical
work speaks'. It is a going back as well as forward. Oldham, Mulgrave,
Roscommon, Granville, and Dryden all wrote poetical 'essays' or 'arts' in
imitation of, or in order to translate, the Horatian *Art of Poetry*.
Dryden's transfusion of Boileau's *Art poétique* re-enacts Boileau's
transplantation of Horace. Rymer discovered his critical relations with
Dryden as poet when, in 1674, he rendered into English Rapin's
Réflexions sur la poétique and praised the beauty and tenderness of
Dryden's description of night.[19] Dryden's lifelong sensitivity to Rymer,
and his generous praise of Rapin as among the 'greatest of this age',
absorb Rapin's reflexive impulse into the whole situation of English
criticism in Dryden's time, and thus (since the past survives into the
present, and nothing is lost out of nature) into the whole situation of
criticism. Without such constants there is no such thing as 'Dryden's
literary criticism', and no concept of criticism beyond the bounds of an
incorrigible present. And without such a concept there is no history of
criticism to be written.

NOTES

1. Howard Erskine-Hill, *Poetry of Opposition and Revolution: Dryden to Wordsworth* (Oxford, 1996), p. 40. According to Paul Hammond, such allusions 'are not jagged shards on an otherwise smooth path: rather they are part of a continuum, an extended meditation on likeness and difference which is sustained by a fundamental fascination with the management of change'. See *Dryden and the Traces of Classical Rome* (Oxford, 1999), p. 149.

2. Editors of Dryden's essays such as George Watson have been selective about what counts as 'criticism' in Dryden, sometimes separating out certain passages which seem 'of critical interest' from the 'work of hack-biography'. See *Of Dramatic Poesy and Other Critical Essays*, edited by George Watson, 2 vols (London, 1962; hereafter '*Essays*'), II, 66.

3. For discussion of this issue see my 'Criticism and the Meanings of "Theory"', *British Journal of Aesthetics*, 37 (1997), 377–85.

4. The difficulty is easily illustrated from standard studies. Robert D. Hume, in *Dryden's Criticism* (Ithaca, 1970), prints 'A Chronological List of Dryden's Major Critical Essays' which admits the 'Life of Plutarch'. Edward Pechter, in *Dryden's Classical Theory of Literature* (Cambridge, 1975), also includes 'literary biography' amongst Dryden's critical work (p. 1).

5. See Collingwood's 'History as Re-Enactment of Past Experience', in *The Idea of History*, edited by Jan van der Dussen (Oxford, 1994), pp. 282–302. Collingwood's conception of 're-enactment' as a basis for knowing the past is discussed in detail by Paul Ricoeur, 'The Reality of the Past', in *Time and Narrative*, translated by Kathleen Blamey and David Pellauer, 3 vols (Chicago, 1988), III, 142–56.

6. Dryden, *Of the Pythagorean Philosophy*, 262–3; Kinsley, IV, 1724.

7. *The Cambridge History of Literary Criticism*, IV: *The Eighteenth Century*, edited by H. B. Nisbet and Claude Rawson (Cambridge, 1997), p. xviii.

8. Kermode recruits Dryden to the cause of those amongst critics of Shakespeare who – like Johnson – have remained 'on this side idolatry'. Preface, *Shakespeare's Language* (London, 2000), p. viii.

9. See, for example, my 'A Dryden Allusion to Rymer's Rapin', *N&Q*, 221 (1976), 554.

10. George Saintsbury, *A History of Criticism and Literary Taste in Europe*, II: *From the Renaissance to the Decline of Eighteenth Century Orthodoxy*, second edition (Edinburgh, 1905), p. 392; J. W. H. Atkins, *English Literary Criticism: Seventeenth and Eighteenth Centuries* (London, 1951), p. 72.

11. Rapin was much translated into English in the 1670s; especially relevant here is John Davies's rendering, *Observations on the Poems of Homer and Vergil* (London, 1672). For Bouhours, whose criticism was not Englished until the early eighteenth century, see *Les entretiens d'Ariste et d'Eugene* and *La manière de bien penser dans les ouvrages d'esprit*.

12. See *The Twickenham Edition of the Poems of Alexander Pope*, VII: *The Iliad of Homer, Books I–IX*, edited by Maynard Mack (New Haven, 1967), pp. 3–25, especially pp. 4–5.

13. *The Yale Edition of the Works of Samuel Johnson*, VII: *Johnson on Shakespeare*, edited by Arthur Sherbo (New Haven, 1968), p. 84.

14. For full details of Johnson's use of Pope here, see my 'Johnson's Life of Pope and Pope's Preface to the *Iliad*', *N&Q* 225 (1980), 50.

15. Most recently, Michael Werth Gelber writes in the concluding chapter of *The Just and the Lively: The Literary Criticism of John Dryden* (New York, 1999) of the 'theoretical' and the 'practical' as the two principal tasks of Dryden's work as a critic (p. 242).

16. R. S. Crane, 'On Writing the History of Criticism in England, 1650–1800' (1953), in *The Idea of the Humanities and Other Essays Critical and Historical*, 2 vols (Chicago, 1967), II, 174–5. Both Hume and Pechter (n. 4) express indebtedness to this essay, but do not, it seems to me, develop its implications for their practice as critical historians.

17. For Collingwood see, for example, *The Idea of History* (n. 6), p. 226: 'By historical thinking, the mind whose self-knowledge is history not only discovers within itself those powers of which historical thought reveals the possession, but actually develops those powers from a latent to an actual state.'

18. Hans-Georg Gadamer, 'The Elevation of the Historicity of Understanding', *Truth and Method*, translation revised by Joel Weinsheimer and Donald G. Marshall, second edition (London, 1989), pp. 289–90.

19. Rymer's translation of Rapin's *Réflexions sur la poétique d'Aristote* was published in 1674. The sense in which critics in this period were 'in dialogue' through the medium of their published works is suggested by Rymer's own occasional unauthorized additions as translator to the 'source' text of Rapin's first edition of the *Réflexions*. Curiously, and for reasons that no one that I am aware of has been able to explain, these were themselves rendered into French in the second edition of the *Réflexions* published in 1675.

'Et versus digitos habet': Dryden, Montaigne, Lucretius, Virgil, and Boccaccio in Praise of Venus

Tom Mason

It has probably never been easy to create a convincingly coherent narrative to contain the various phenomena that are the product of Dryden's writing life. It is, perhaps, particularly difficult to present his poems to non-specialists in such a way that his *œuvre* can be seen to resemble those of other poets whose creative powers are highly esteemed. The suggestion that Dryden did not produce a self-defining, culminating masterpiece might meet with general assent – now that exclusive contemplation of *Absalom and Achitophel* has come to seem restrictive. And there might well seem to be something odd about a poet who gave so much of his time at the height of his powers to translating the works of others – of so many and such various others. For some readers in the nineteenth and twentieth centuries Dryden seemed to be a purely mercenary poet, willing and able to turn his hand to whatever the age demanded or the market would support (his cause may not have been helped by the concentration of so much of the eighteenth-century praise on his diction and versification). To counter such charges, it has been claimed that the poems Dryden chose to translate spoke to him about his present position – or were *made* to speak of it. The easiest things to point to are political references, half-hidden jokes, and so on – the felicity of his making Juvenal in his Third Satire describe himself as 'Maimed, and unuseful to the government', say, or his making Ovid's Pythagoras compare the flux of years to 'abdicated Kings'. That Dryden discovered much *from* his translations as well as bringing thought *to* them is more difficult to establish. Arguably, it remains an open question whether translation was for Dryden a purely literary exercise, the result of a temporary enthusiasm, or in some sense a transforming experience, an education, an encountering.

One interesting but comparatively minute case which may shed some light on some of these problems involves two passages of which Dryden included translations in his 1685 collection *Sylvae*. They are the passage from Book VIII of the *Æneid* (387–406) in which Venus seduces her

husband Vulcan in order to persuade him to make some armour for
Æneas, and the opening of Lucretius' *De Rerum Natura* (1–40), in which
Lucretius beseeches Venus to seduce her lover Mars in order that the
world may have peace and he may write his great poem. By pure chance,
a letter from Dryden to his publisher survives which suggests that
Dryden was led to connect these passages by Montaigne's essay 'Upon
Some Verses of Virgil'.[1] Dryden appears to assume that Tonson will
recognize the passages and will appreciate the connection between the
lines from Lucretius and those from Virgil, and he implies that the
connection between them is the reason for their inclusion in *Sylvae*.
There have, that is, always been good *prima facie* reasons for thinking
that Dryden's interest in these passages followed or flowed from
Montaigne's interest; that Dryden read with thoughts and feelings in
some consonance with Montaigne's.

Several commentators have argued that Dryden's relations with
Montaigne represented, or were the result of, a sympathy of spirit rather
than a surface resemblance of thought, a sympathy reaching down to
Dryden's deepest feelings.[2] It seems that Dryden's thoughts returned on
a variety of apparently disparate occasions to Montaigne's essay 'Upon
Some Verses of Virgil', including the Latin lines there discussed,
particularly at the very end of his life. As is almost invariably the case in
Dryden's translations, the process of rendering one author involved an
admixture with another, or with many others – sometimes creating
strange bedfellows. Paul Hammond's edition (*Poems*, II, 208–11) shows
how some lines from Spenser and many passages from *Paradise Lost*
came into Dryden's mind on his first turning to the Lucretius passage
discussed in Montaigne's essay. This combination of Lucretius,
Montaigne, and Spenser recurred to him when he turned to some
passages of the story told by the Knight in the *Canterbury Tales*. Some
of Montaigne's thoughts seem to have mingled with those that came into
his mind when reading and rendering Boccaccio. One indication that
these associations were not merely idiosyncratic and peculiar to Dryden
is suggested by the fact that when Alexander Pope came to some
passages in the *Iliad* he retraced much of the path Dryden had travelled,
as I shall attempt to demonstrate. A line of transmission – certainly of
words, possibly of thoughts – would seem to run from Montaigne
(reading Lucretius and Virgil) to Dryden (taking in Milton and Spenser,
Chaucer, and Boccaccio) to Pope (taking in Milton and Homer).

In the Preface to his *Dictionary* Samuel Johnson justified his inclusion
of several illustrations of the same word by maintaining that the practice
would show 'how one author copied the thoughts and diction of
another', so providing 'a kind of intellectual history', or a 'genealogy of

sentiments'. The source or spring of the miniature intellectual history with which I am concerned can perhaps be located in the notes of the *editio princeps* of *De Rerum Natura*, edited by Denis Lambin and published in 1563. Lambinus' commentary establishes a series of parallels between Lucretius' diction and Virgil's, demonstrating the indebtedness of the later to the earlier Latin poet (and, in one early note, suggesting a common debt to Ennius). For example, in his note to the word *devinctus* (as it appears in Lucretius' phrase 'aeterno devinctus volnere amoris', 'fettered and vanquished by the eternal wound of love') Lambinus compares a line from Book VIII of the *Æneid* ('Tum pater aeterno fatur devinctus amore', 'then spoke the godhead, fettered by immortal love'), and suggests that the reference in both cases is to the episode in Homer's *Odyssey* when Aphrodite and Ares, caught in the act of adultery, are enmeshed in Hephaestus' net of fine chain.[3]

A few years ago, a copy of Lambinus' Lucretius which appears to have been owned by Montaigne turned up in the lists of an antiquarian dealer.[4] The marginalia and annotations to the flyleaves suggest that Montaigne (if the hand is his) read through the whole poem in a few months of the year 1564 with intense and wide-ranging attention. As far as can be gathered, Montaigne's interest seems to have been sometimes in the philosophy, sometimes in miscellaneous facts, sometimes in the poetry. Occasionally he seems to have been attending to all of these at once. This volume's annotations, then, apparently trace the beginnings of a continuing and profound interest in Lucretius' poem (there are more quotations from Lucretius in Montaigne's *Essays* than from any other poet).[5] For the purposes of the present argument, the important pen marks are those on the opening pages of Lucretius' poem. On page 5 Montaigne wrote 'Amors de mars / & Venus' and 'imité par Vergil', and put pen strokes (apparently marks of extreme approbation) in the inner margin against the last seven lines describing the wished-for seduction of Mars.

Years later, when Montaigne proposed to himself an essay on human sexuality, these passages came into his mind as points of departure and return. The evidence of his copy of Lambinus' edition (if it is that) suggests that Montaigne worked hard at his studies. The evidence of his essay suggests that he was also to the highest degree engaged and enraptured by both these passages of Latin poetry. For, although Virgil and Lucretius play only a small part in the essay (which draws most frequently on Catullus, Ovid, and Martial), it is their passages in praise of Venus that are given most weight. The connection between them appears to be partly that the Lucretius is the source, or, as he puts it, 'mother', of the later poem, but most importantly, though less precisely, that the two passages demonstrate similar qualities in the writing, and present or suggest, hint at or imply, a common view of sexuality – human and divine.

So far and so wide does this essay saunter, so many are its shifts of subject, focus, and mood, that it is not easy to say quite what constitutes its centre. So many are the shades of tone, from the playful to the passionate, that the essay is not susceptible to paraphrase or summary. Most of Montaigne's speculations, however, seem to spring from the position in which he writes – that of an old man reviving his spirits by busying and diverting his mind 'in wanton and youthful Thoughts' as an antidote to age, which every day reads him 'new Lectures of Coldness and Temperance'.[6] He presents himself as having, like Horace, weathered the storms of love, hung his wet clothes in the temple of Neptune, and as therefore able to contemplate the storms of love from the safety of the shore (p. 117). In this essay Montaigne sees himself as taking one last look at some of his favourite Latin verses on the subject of love, and half-comically taking leave of the pleasures of Venus – almost of life itself: 'In farewels, we above ordinary heat our Affections towards the things we leave of. I take my last leave of the pleasures of this World, these are our last embraces' (p. 101).

One of Montaigne's leading suggestions is that the force and power of Venus are more clearly seen in poetry than in life – and seen most clearly of all in her effects on the imaginations of an old man:

> Wither'd and drooping as I am, I feel yet some remains of that past ardour ... But from what I understand of it, the force and power of this *God* are more lively and animating in the Picture of Poesie than in their own Essence,
>
> *Et versus digitos habet:*
>
> It has, I know not what kind of air, more amorous than Love itself; *Venus* is not so beautiful, naked, alive, and panting, as she is here in *Virgil*.
>
> (p. 104)

Montaigne's tag 'Et versus digitos habet' was translated by Cotton with uncharacteristic prudery: 'For there is charming harmony in Verse'. It is an adaptation of the words from Juvenal's Satire VI (describing the effect of Roman women making love in Greek) that may have been used by Montaigne with some of the force that Dryden was to give them in his version – those 'tender words', he calls them, which the 'momentary trembling bliss affords', the 'kind soft murmurs of the private sheets':

> Those words have fingers, and their force is such,
> They raise the dead, and mount him with a touch.[7]

Montaigne appears to be implying that Virgil's lines are straight-forwardly erotic, even sexually stimulating. They are more erotic than anything that real life has offered, or might offer – certainly to a man of his years.

It is perhaps not easy for modern readers to apply such phrases, or such notions, either to the Latin, or to Dryden's rendering – where the emphasis seems to be less on the provocative power of the moment than on the speed with which desire is infused into Vulcan and the self-conscious artifice of the 'wiles' of Venus:

> Dixerat; et niveis, hinc atque hinc Diva lacertis
> Cunctantem amplexu molli fovet. Ille repente
> Accepit solitam flammam; notusque medullas
> Intravit calor, et labefacta per ossa cucurrit.
> Non secus atque olim tonitru cum rupta corusco
> Ignea rima micans percurrit lumine nimbos.
>   ... Ea verba loquutus,
> Optatos dedit amplexus, placidumque petivit
> Conjugis infusus gremio per membra soporem

> She said; and straight her arms of snowy hue
> About her unresolving husband threw;
> Her soft embraces soon infuse desire,
> His bones and marrow suddain warmth inspire,
> And all the godhead feels the wonted fire.
> Not half so swift the rowling thunder flies,
> Or streaks of lightning flash along the skies.
> The goddess, pleased with her successful wiles,
> And conscious of her conquering beauty, smiles.
> Then thus the good old god, soothed with her charms,
> Panting, and half dissolving in her arms:
> 'Why seek you reasons for a Cause so just,
> Or your own beauty, or my love distrust? ...'
> He said; and eager to enjoy her charms
> He snatched the lovely goddess to his arms;
> Till all infused in joy he lay possessed
> Of full desire, and sunk to pleasing rest.
>   (28–40, 51–4; *Poems*, II, 304–5)

Montaigne follows his remarks on Virgil with a lengthy complaint
that Venus and Vulcan are altogether too amorous for a married couple,
since love and marriage have little in common. Virgil has 'represented
her a little too Passionate for a married *Venus*. In this discreet kind of
coupling, the Appetite is not usually so wanton, but more grave and dull'
(Cotton, p. 105). For Montaigne these deities are godlike partly or
largely in their freedom from embarrassment or jealousy: 'Our Poet
represents Marriage happy in good intelligence, wherin nevertheless
there is not much Loyalty' (p. 112). Venus is unafraid to seek her husband's
help for her illegitimate son, the result of one of many adulterous liaisons
with gods and mortal men. Vulcan is happy to provide that help: 'nay
she entreats Arms for a Bastard of hers ... which are freely granted; and
Vulcan speaks honourably of *Æneas* ... with, in truth, a more than
humane Humanity' (pp. 131–2). Although, in Dryden's rendering of
these lines in 'The Speech of Venus to Vulcan' in *Sylvae*, Vulcan speaks
as honourably of *Æneas'* *cause* as of the man, and the brevity of the god's
hurried reply slides the whole scene towards the comic rather than the
erotic, Dryden's epithet for Vulcan, 'good old god' (37), might well seem
to be a phrase coined in the spirit of Montaigne's 'more than humane
humanity'. Indeed, a case might be made that in his first engagement
with the passage Dryden was responding more to Montaigne than to
Virgil. When he rewrote the passage in 1697 as part of his translation of
the whole *Æneid*, the 'good old god' became the more dignified 'Power'
(*Poems*, II, 304 supplies both versions).

It is much later in his essay that Montaigne turns to the passage from
Lucretius. Again, his introductory remarks draw attention to the
unconventionality of the union. His preference for Lucretius seems to
rest partly on its being a depiction of Venus' power over a lover rather
than a husband: 'What *Virgil* says of *Venus* and *Vulcan*, *Lucretius* had
better express'd of a stolen enjoyment betwixt her and *Mars*' (Cotton, p.
146). Montaigne assumes that both passages have the same subject, and
that his preference for Lucretius is uncontentious:

> Belli fera moenera Mavors
> Armipotens regit, in gremium qui saepe tuum se
> Rejicit, aeterno devinctus vulnere amoris: ...
> Pascit amore avidos inhians in te Dea visus,
> Eque tuo pendet resupini spiritus ore:
> Hunc tu Diva tuo recubantem corpore sancto
> Circumfusa super, suaveis ex ore loquelas
> Funde.

the brutal business of the war
Is managed by thy dreadful servant's care:
Who oft retires from fighting fields to prove
The pleasing pains of thy eternal love,
And panting on thy breast supinely lies,
While with thy heavenly form he feeds his famished eyes,
Sucks in with open lips thy balmy breath,
By turns restored to life, and plunged in pleasing death.
There while thy curling limbs about him move,
Involv'd and fettered in the links of love,
When wishing all he nothing can deny,
Thy charms in that auspicious moment try

(*Poems*, II, 31)

It is impossible to know whether Dryden shared this preference. But readers of Dryden have found a peculiar felicity in this translation from Lucretius, and have suggested that it called forth his highest powers. As several commentators have pointed out, the strongest praise of this translation on record is that of John Wilson ('Christopher North'), the nineteenth-century critic and early admirer of Wordsworth, who claimed that the passage 'may compete with any piece of translation in the language'. Wilson assumed that the passage must have been written in one of Dryden's 'happiest veins', and that Dryden 'was called to his task by desire ... under the sting of the poetical oestrum'.[8] (Wilson does not make clear whether he assumes the desire in question was stimulated by a purely poetic interest, or one that resembled sexual desire.)

Where the passage from Virgil had led Montaigne into large speculations on love and marriage, the concentration of Montaigne's remarks immediately following his quotation from Lucretius is upon the power of the Latin as poetry, and in particular on the power of the diction – upon the power of certain words in certain combinations:

Quand je rumine ce, *rejicit, pascit, inhians, molli, fovet, medullas, labefacta, pendet, percurrit*, et cette noble *circumfusa*, mere du gentil *infusus*, j'ay desdain de ces menues pointes et allusions verballes, qui nasquirent depuis. A ces bonnes gens, il ne falloit pas d'aiguë et subtile rencontre: Leur langage est tout plein, et gros d'une vigueur naturelle et constante: Ils sont tout epigramme, non la queue seulement, mais la teste, l'estomach, et les pieds. Il n'y a rien d'efforcé, rien de treinant: tout y marche d'une pareille teneur. *Contextus totus virilis est, non sunt circa flosculos occupati.* Ce n'est pas une eloquence molle et seulement sans offense: elle est

nerveuse et solide, qui ne plaist pas tant, comme elle remplit et
ravit: et ravit le plus les plus forts espris. Quand je voy ces braves
formes de s'expliquer, si vifves, si profondes, je ne dicts pas que
c'est bien dire, je dicts que c'est bien penser. C'est la gaillardise de
l'imagination, que esleve et enfle les parolles. *Pectus est quod
disertum facit.* Nos gens appellent jugement, langage, et beaux
mots, les pleines conceptions. Cette peinture est conduite, non tant
par dexterité de la main, comme pour avoir l'object plus vifvement
empreint en l'ame.[9]

Montaigne discusses the two passages almost as if they were one –
pointing in particular to the vigour of the shared vocabulary when
compared with any available to him in a modern vernacular:

> When I consider this *rejicit, pascit, inhians, molli, fovet, medullas,
> labefacta, pendet, percurrit,* and that noble *circumfusa,* mother of the
> gentle *infusus;* I contemn those little Quibbles and verbal Allusions
> that have been since in use.
>
> (Cotton, pp. 146–7)

It is not clear whether Montaigne wants to consider the words
themselves or his thoughts about them – or whether the two are separable.
These words seem to act more directly upon his mind than the thing
contemplated. If the words of Virgil had the power to stir with the
fingers of desire, the words of Virgil and Lucretius combined have
power to ravish the mind:

> There is nothing forc'd, nothing languishing, but they still keep
> the same pace ... 'Tis not a soft Eloquence, and without offence
> only; 'tis nervous and solid, that does not so much please, as it fills
> and ravishes the greatest minds.
>
> (p. 147)

This description of the force and ravishing power of poetry resembles
what Dryden and Pope say in praise of Homer. The verb 'fills' in 'it fills
and ravishes the greatest minds' is Cotton's expansion of the French.
Montaigne appears to assume that when in the presence of poetry he is
in the presence of thought, or 'mind':

> When I see these brave forms of expression, so lively, so profound,
> I do not say that 'tis well said, but well thought. 'Tis the
> sprightliness of the imagination that swells and elevates the words.

> *Pectus est quod disertum facit* ... This painting is not so much
> carried on by dexterity of hand, as by having the object more lively
> imprinted in the Soul.
>
> (p. 147)

Montaigne was making a remarkable claim: that so vividly were these
words imprinted in the poet's soul that they seem to have bodies and
actually to live: 'the Sense illuminates and produces the words: no mere
words of air, but of flesh and bone; they signify more than they express'
(p. 148).

It is hard to know exactly what Montaigne understood by the words
he singled out from Virgil and Lucretius miscellaneously, or exactly why
these particular ones ravished his mind. Some of Lucretius' words were
commented upon by Lambinus, others not. Montaigne acknowledges
that they may have lost some of their force by having become, as it were,
hereditary: 'Of some of the words I have picked out ... we do not so
easily discern the energy, by reason that the frequent use of them has in
some sort abased their beauty, and rendered it common' (Cotton, p.
149). It is the 'handling and utterance' of Virgil and Lucretius that
distinguishes their language from that of other poets –

> not so much by innovating it, as by putting it to more vigorous and
> various, service, and by straining, bending, and adapting it to
> them. They do not create words, but they enrich their own, and
> give them weight and signification by the Uses they put them to,
> and teach them unwonted motions, but withall, ingeniously and
> discreetly.
>
> (p. 148)

In his version of the Venus and Vulcan episode from Virgil, Dryden
seems to have chosen words not obviously far removed from common
use. He does not appear to have bent or adapted the common vocabulary
in any particular direction. Nor can it be said with certainty that Dryden
responded to these particular words more than others. Virgil's word
rejicit, for example, may have been transferred from Vulcan to Venus, as
it were, and have suggested Dryden's description of the goddess
'throwing' her arms 'about her unresolving husband'. Although that
phrase does not seem to have been as common as it has since become,
Dryden might appear to have done little to put it to 'more vigorous and
various, service, and by straining, bending, and adapting it'. Similarly
when he came to the word *medullas* and wrote:

> Her soft embraces soon infuse desire,
> His bones and marrow suddain warmth inspire

Dryden seems to have done little more than to recall Cowley's poem, 'The Thraldome':

> I *Came*, I *Saw*, and was *undone*;
> *Lightning* did through my bones and marrow run;
> A *pointed pain* pierc'd deep my heart;
> A swift, cold trembling seiz'd on every part[10]

But to the passage from Lucretius, Dryden appears to have brought a vocabulary and an accompanying range of thoughts quite different from Montaigne, whose interest seems to be exclusively in the seduction of Mars. For Dryden, the opening of *De Rerum Natura* appears to have been a hymn or a prayer rather than an erotic description. For example, as the California edition hints, Dryden seems to have expanded everything in the Latin that makes the passage a prayer for peace – a universal, absolute freedom from barbarous discord:

> Delight of human kind and gods above,
> Parent of Rome, propitious Queen of love,
> Whose vital power air, earth and sea supplies,
> And breeds whate'er is born beneath the rolling skies ...
> Be thou my aid: my tuneful song inspire,
> And kindle with thy own productive fire; ...
> With winning eloquence our peace implore,
> And quiet to the weary world restore.
> (1–4, 32–3, 57–8; Poems, II, 308–11)[11]

For Dryden these verses appear to have had elegance, rather than fingers. Paul Hammond has suggested that Dryden's was 'concerned to achieve a formal beauty', a formality that can be seen in the 'decorous repetitions' that Dryden adapted from Spenser's version of the passage'.[12] And the elegance is of a comparatively simple kind. Much of the opening passage appears to be organized (as it had been by Spenser) around the direct imitation of the Latin invocation: 'te, Dea, te', 'Thee, Goddess, Thee':

> Thee, goddess, thee the clouds and tempests fear,
> And at thy pleasing presence disappear;

> For thee the land in fragrant flowers is dressed,
> For thee the ocean smiles, and smooths her wavy breast,
> And heaven itself with more serene and purer light is blessed.
>
> (7–12; *Poems*, II, 309)

It is perhaps significant that when in *Palamon and Arcite* Dryden came to Palamon's prayer, he returned as much to Spenser as to Lucretius:

> For thee the Winds their Eastern Blasts forbear,
> Thy Month reveals the Spring, and opens all the Year.
> Thee, Goddess, thee the Storms of Winter fly,
> Earth smiles with Flow'rs renewing; laughs the Sky,
> And Birds to Lays of Love their tuneful Notes apply.
> For thee the Lion loathes the Taste of Blood,
> And roaring hunts his Female through the Wood:
> For thee the Bulls rebellow through the Groves,
> And Tempt the Stream, and snuff their absent Loves.
> 'Tis thine, whate'er is pleasant, good, or fair:
> All Nature is thy Province, Life thy Care;
> Thou mad'st the World, and dost the World repair.
>
> (IV, 133–44; Kinsley, IV, 1503–4)

It might also be said that Dryden is more interested than Montaigne in Venus as a universal power. The description of Venus' seduction of Mars is the culmination of a larger whole. John Mason has pointed to a list of words that are not found in Dryden's predecessor-translators, Creech and Evelyn, but seem to have a similar force in Dryden's passage to Montaigne's list in the Latin poems: 'vital power', 'breeds', 'every kind', 'prolifique might', 'springs', 'fragrant', 'teeming', 'joyous', 'genial fire', 'bound', 'strook', 'various progeny', 'stung with delight', 'goaded', 'uncontroul'd', 'boundless', and 'wondrous'. All these words, he argues, carry something of the charge they were given in *Paradise Lost*, and forge a 'real link between delight in nature and delight in copulation'.[13] Dryden, it might be said, has emphasized (with Spenser) everything that makes Lucretius' passage a prayer to a goddess whose 'force and power' is equally present in the created world and in the details of the act of copulation, human and divine.

However, such an interest is not entirely foreign to Montaigne. The general praise of the power of Venus is given marks of approbation in the margins of his copy of Lambinus, and, in the essay, he invented a line ('Tu, Dea, tu rerum naturam sola gubernas') constructed from fragments of Lucretius' hymn to Venus' general power to emphasize as

support for the suggestion that thoughts of love are as essential to the
Muses of Poetry as generation and propagation are to the natural world
(p. 102), and that 'All the motions in the World tend to this Conjunction;
'tis a matter infus'd throughout: 'tis a Center to which all things tend'
(p. 119). And if Dryden's set of key words is not quite the same as
Montaigne's, there are some instances where Dryden's vocabulary does
seem to represent a response to Lucretius that was shared with (if not
directed by) Montaigne – though a response that takes various and
divergent forms. When, for example, Montaigne singled out 'the gentle
infusus' from Virgil, he does seem to have struck a chord with Dryden,
in that Dryden simply tears the word out of Latin to plant it in his
English verse three times (though in three different senses), twice
without prompting from the Latin – first when describing the first
effects of Venus' blandishments in 'The Speech of Venus to Vulcan':

> Her soft embraces soon infuse desire
> (30)

and then to evoke Venus' wished-for effects on his poem in the
Lucretian exordium:

> assist my Muse and me
> Infusing verses worthy him and thee.
> (39–40)[14]

Dryden's response to 'that noble *circumfusa*, mother of the gentle *infusus*'
appears to have taken an opposite direction. If he does not exactly
innovate, he puts a common word to 'more vigorous and various service',
by 'straining, bending, and adapting' it.[15] In his version, Lucretius begs
Venus to ask Mars for peace at the auspicious moment

> while thy curling limbs about him move,
> Involved and fettered in the links of love.
> (53–4; *Poems*, II, 331)

Dryden's use of the word 'curling' as some kind of representation of the
word *circumfusa* has been decried by Norman Austin, who accused
Dryden of being 'deliberately wanton', and defended by Paul Hammond,
who thought Dryden's manner 'not prurient, but delighted, with the
good sense that Chaucer or Montaigne can bring to the subject'.[16]

   Dryden may have been striving for a sexual vocabulary that exactly
matched Montaigne's observations (or prescriptions). As Montaigne

read them, Virgil and Lucretius are forceful and stimulating because, in treating so 'reservedly and discreetly' of 'wantonness', they 'discover it much more openly' and draw us on (Cotton, p. 159). Ovid, by contrast, is over-explicit. Montaigne is *'eunuch'd'* with the plainness of that poet's expression in the line 'Et nudum pressi corpus ad usque meum'. Even Martial may 'turn up *Venus*' coats as high' as he can without displaying her as nakedly as Lucretius and Virgil, who 'open ... so fair a path to Imagination', had done (p. 160). Dryden may have thought of Venus' 'curling limbs' similarly – as words that involved readers' minds actively rather than presenting them with a picture to be viewed with prurience or in passivity.

Although not a 'borrowing' from Milton, the idea, as it were, *behind* the word 'curling' may derive from the description of Eve's 'unadorned golden tresses' which in 'wanton ringlets wav'd', as 'the Vine curles her tendrils'.[17] Dryden used the word again – but altogether more actively – when, in his version of Chaucer's *Knight's Tale*, Arcite prays to Mars and beseeches the God to have pity on his 'pains', pains that were Mars' own when the 'yielded' Venus 'lay curling' in his 'arms' (318; Kinsley, IV, 1508). The imagination must necessarily be employed in understanding this use of the word. *OED* quotes Dryden's line as an instance of the sense (5a) 'To take a spiral or incurved form or posture', but it would seem to be closer to sense 7, 'To move in spiral convolutions or undulations'. Something of what Dryden may have had in mind can be gathered from a moment in the *Memoirs of a Woman of Pleasure* when Cleland made the connection with Milton:

> ... he laid his naked glowing body to mine: —— Oh insupportable delight! oh superhumane rapture! ... curling round him like the tendril of a vine, as if I fear'd any part of him should be untouch'd or unpress'd by me; I return'd his strenuous embraces and kisses with a fervour and gust only known to true love.[18]

A second instance (a development, perhaps, of the range of thoughts suggested by '*infusus* daughter of the noble *circumfusa*') is presented by the rhyme 'possest'/'rest' – as in the conclusion of the passage from Virgil. Vulcan, 'eager to enjoy' the 'charms' of Venus, 'snatch'd the lovely Goddess to his arms',

> Till all infus'd in joy he lay possest
> Of full desire, and sunk to pleasing rest.
> (54–5; *Poems*, II, 305)

Slight as it may seem, the detail that seems to have been operative in Dryden's mind was that of the god 'sinking'. In *Alexander's Feast*, as Timotheus begins to sing of love, Alexander 'Gazed on the fair / Who caused his care, / And sighed and looked, sighed and looked, / Sighed and looked, and sighed again', until

> At length, with Love and Wine at once oppress'd,
> The vanquish'd Victor sunk upon her Breast.
>   (114–15; Kinsley, III, 1431)

Here Dryden appears to be using the word 'opprest' as it had been used in Book IX of *Paradise Lost*, when, after the fall, Adam and Eve 'Took largely' their 'Fill of Love and Love's disport' till 'dewie sleep / Oppress'd them, weary with thir amorous play' (1042–5).

All these passages seem to have come into Alexander Pope's mind when, translating Book XIV of the *Iliad*, he arrived at what he regarded as 'one of the most beautiful Pieces that ever was produc'd by Poetry', the 'congress' of Jupiter and Juno. When Jupiter, seduced by Juno (in order to further her cause) falls asleep, Pope recalled Dryden's Alexander ('at length with love ... oppress'd') alongside Dryden's Vulcan ('sunk to rest'):

> At length with Love and Sleep's soft Pow'r opprest,
> The panting Thund'rer nods, and sinks to Rest.[19]

Has Pope encapsulated the soul of the matter, picked up and concentrated the leading thought that Dryden learned from or shared with Montaigne? One feature that the passages describing the 'congress' of Venus and Vulcan, Venus and Mars, and Juno and Jove, have (or were seen to have) in common is that the male deity (or, if Alexander's case is included, a 'godlike man') is obliterated, dissolved, consumed, enervated, extinguished. The pleasure offered is perhaps that of seeing human frailties amplified to the greatest possible scale – of seeing the most powerful rulers of the universe display a 'more than humane humanity'. The suggestion seems almost to be that the greatest happiness a male (god or man) can know is that of sinking to oblivion while possessed of full desire and being well-deceived. That which makes a man godlike is his utter subservience to the obliterating power of Venus – or, as Pope had Homer put it in *Iliad* XIV,

> those conqu'ring Charms,
> That Pow'r, which Mortals and Immortals warms,

That Love, which melts Mankind in fierce Desires,
And burns the Sons of Heav'n with sacred Fires.

(225–8)

For Montaigne, Dryden, and Pope, these passages seem to have represented a peculiarly poetical way of giving form to a power that is distinctly and triumphantly female. The force and power of Venus is partly the force and power of her sexual attractions, and partly the cunning of her wiles. Venus, and Juno (wearing the *cestus* of Venus), triumph over Vulcan, Mars, and Jupiter in a way that is rendered as delightful to the reader as to the god.

As Montaigne presents the matter, Venus' freedoms are proper because sexual desire and sexual performance have their natural seat in female form. Venus is a goddess, perhaps, in that she *can* do what mortal women *should* do: 'Tis folly ... to attempt to bridle in Women a Desire that is so powerful in them, and so natural to them' (Cotton, p. 135). Dryden does not seem to have shared this thought when writing the versions for *Sylvae*. There the concentration is upon male desire. Venus enjoys only her conquests. One minute alteration between the 1685 and 1687 versions of the passage from Virgil, however, may suggest a new direction. In *Sylvae*, Vulcan 'snatched the lovely goddess to his arms'. In the complete translation, the lovely goddess becomes 'willing' (*Poems*, II, 305). In Virgil the 'amplexus' is 'optatos': the embraces are ambiguously wished-for.

It was not, however, until turning to Boccaccio that Dryden gave shape to this side of Montaigne's thought. One leading suggestion of Montaigne's essay is that mortal men, unlike immortal gods, are absurd in attempting to impose a set of impossible restrictions upon the minds and actions of women, 'the Usurpation of sovereign Authority ... over the Women' (p. 175):

> Women are not to blame at all, when they refuse the Rules of Life that are introduc'd into the World, forasmuch as the Men made them without their Consent. There is naturally Contention and Brawling between them and us; and the strictest Friendship we have with them, is yet mixed with Tumult and Tempest.
>
> (pp. 113–14)

Richard Bates points out that Dryden appears to have recalled the very words of Cotton's translation ('usurpation', and 'without their consent') when coming to the daughter's defence in his 1700 version of Boccaccio's tale of *Sigismonda and Guiscardo*.[20] Sigismonda defends her

actions by complaining of Tancred's 'little Care to mend' her 'Widow'd
Nights' (414). What has she 'done in this, deserving Blame', she asks:
'Nature's' laws are eternal, while 'State-Laws may alter', and are

> usurp'd on helpless Woman-kind,
> Made without our Consent, and wanting Pow'r to bind.
> (Kinsley, IV, 1556)

According to Montaigne, one reason the male state-laws have no power
to bind women is the strength of their sexual capacities – sexual
capacities that are given by nature and fostered by the very upbringing
that is designed to suppress them. Dryden departed from Boccaccio to
write of Sigismonda that 'Youth, Health, and Ease, and most an amorous
Mind, / To second Nuptials had her Thoughts inclin'd' (34–5), coming
close to Montaigne's remark that the 'good Instructors, Nature, Youth
and Health', are 'continually inspiring' women with a propensity for love
(p. 119).

Perhaps the most surprising moment in Montaigne's essay is its
conclusion:

> I say that Males and Females are cast in the same Mould, and that,
> Education and Usage excepted, the difference is not great ... It is
> much more easy to accuse one Sex than to excuse the other; 'Tis
> according to the Proverb, *Ill may Vice correct Sin.*
> (Cotton, pp. 189–90)

Dryden's Sigismonda presents herself as cast in the same 'mould' as her
parent – only, as it were, more so. Montaigne's sentiments are given a
sharp edge when spoken by a daughter to her father:

> as thy Father gave thee Flesh and blood,
> So gav'st thou me: Not from the Quarry Hew'd,
> But of a softer Mould, with Sense endu'd;
> Ev'n softer than thy own, of suppler Kind,
> More exquisite of Taste, and more than Man refin'd.
> (422–6; Kinsley, IV, 1556)

Part of the force of Sigismonda's onslaught on her father is that he, being
old, has forgotten the power and force of the goddess:

> Though now thy sprightly Blood with Age be cold,
> Thou hast been young; and canst remember still,

That when thou hadst the Pow'r, thou hadst the Will;
And from the past Experience of thy Fires,⎫
Canst tell with what a Tide our strong Desires⎬
Come rushing on in Youth, and what their Rage requires.⎭
(428–33; Kinsley, IV, 1556)

Montaigne's half-amused, half-ashamed sense of the unworthiness of an old man to participate in sexual activities colours everything in his essay. It seems to him almost a cruelty in Nature that 'having rendered this age miserable' she should make it 'ridiculous'. His sense of the ridiculous is centred in his genital: 'I hate to see it, for one poor inch of pitiful vigour, which comes upon it but thrice a Week, to strut, and set out itself with as much eagerness as if it could do mighty feats ... and wonder to see it so boyl and bubble' (p. 173). And yet he presents himself as not 'so long cashiered from the state and service of this god, that my memory is not still perfect in his force and value': 'wither'd and drooping' as he is, he still feels 'some remains of that past ardour' (p. 103).

Richard Bates has drawn attention to the general similarities between Montaigne's sentiments and Dryden's 'Poeta loquitur' introducing *Cymon and Iphigenia* (and rebutting Collier's charge of lubricity), and in particular to the possibility that Dryden's unfitness for love is physical:[21]

Old as I am, for Ladies love unfit,
The Pow'r of Beauty I remember yet,
Which once inflam'd my Soul, and still inspires my Wit.
(1–3; Kinsley, IV, 1741)

Dryden's distinction between an inflamed soul and an inspired wit seems also to be in accord with Montaigne's thought – one that (as was mentioned earlier) was derived from (or supported by) Lucretius' general praise of Venus, and of poetry inspired by Venus:

Who will deprive the Muses of amorous Imaginations, will rob them of the best Entertainment they have, and of the noblest matter of their Work: and who will make *Love* lose the Communication and Service of *Poesie*, will disarm him of his best Arms.
(Cotton, p. 103)

It is one of Montaigne's most surprising contentions that love is a more useful force in inspiring the wit of the old than in enflaming the young. As he puts it, however, it is the sleeping soul itself that memories of Venus awaken in the old:

I look upon it as wholesome, and proper to enliven a drowsie Soul,
and to rouze up a heavy Body. And, as an experience'd physician,
I would prescribe it to a man of my form and condition, as soon as
any other *Recipe* whatever to rouze and keep him in vigour till well
advanced in years, and to defer the approaches of Age, whilst we
are but in the Suburbs, and that the Pulse yet beats ... Do but
observe what Youth, Vigour, and Gayety it inspir'd *Anacreon* withal.
(Cotton, p. 180)

Part of Dryden's rejoinder to his puritanical critics in *Cymon and
Iphigenia* is to claim that love is not 'always of a vicious kind' but

> Awakes the sleepy Vigour of the Soul,
> And, brushing o'er, adds Motion to the Pool.
> (29–30; Kinsley, IV, 1742)

The movement of Dryden's thought is almost identical to that of the
essay – from love's power to stir the souls of the old, to the particular
causative relation between love and poetry:

> Love first invented Verse, and form'd the Rhime,
> The Motion measur'd, harmoniz'd the Chime
> (33–4)

Dryden's attribution of moral force to Love, though a commonplace,
may owe something to Montaigne's fancy that, should he re-indulge in
the passion,

> Love would ... restore to me Vigilancy, Sobriety, Grace, and the
> care of my Person ... would again put me upon sound and wise
> studies, by which I might render my self more lov'd and esteem'd,
> clearing my mind of the despair of it self ... and redintigrating it
> to it self.
>
> (p. 183)

> Love, studious how to please, improves our Parts
> With polish'd Manners, and adorns with Arts ...
> To lib'ral Acts inlarg'd the narrow-soul'd:
> Soften'd the fierce, and made the Coward Bold
> (31–2, 35–6; Kinsley, IV, 1742)

Montaigne's case depends on the proposition that 'there is nothing in us during this earthly Prison that is purely either corporeal or spiritual' (p. 181). It is part of Dryden's claim for Love that mind and body are interdependent, so that in this tale from Boccaccio 'all the fair may find, / When beauty fires the blood, how love exalts the mind' (41).

The connection Dryden's mind made between Lucretius and Montaigne is suggested by the closing lines of the 'Poeta Loquitur':

> The World when wast, he Peopled with increase,
> And warring Nations reconcil'd in Peace.
>
> (37–8)

For, although the (male) deity appealed to here is not quite Lucretius' goddess, the last line may be a recollection of that poet's final appeal to Venus to try her winning eloquence to implore our peace and restore quiet to the weary World. In the 'Life of Waller' Samuel Johnson maintained that 'from poetry the reader justly expects, and from good poetry always obtains, the enlargement of his comprehension and elevation of his fancy' (*Lives*, I, 292). These effects, the enlargement of comprehension and elevation of fancy, seem to have been experienced as realities in equal measure by Montaigne and Dryden. Dryden's reading of Lucretius through the eyes of Montaigne seems to have produced or encouraged a continuing meditation on the sexual relations between men and women, and the relationship between sexual desire and the poetic impulse. By the end of his life, love recalled in old age appears to have become as much or more of a poetic impulse than emotion recollected in tranquillity is supposed to have been for Wordsworth. A few lines of Latin verse, connected with some saunteringly diffuse remarks from Montaigne, had so worked in Dryden's mind that they had come to represent the essence (or one of the possible essences) of his art, his inspiration.

But the 'Poeta Loquitur' at the opening of *Cymon and Iphiginea* cannot be said to represent a point of conclusion. Dryden was perhaps investing no more in these lines than did Montaigne in any single paragraph or proposition. (It is hard to see the love that infects Cymon as beneficent.) Johnson distinguished Dryden and Pope with the claim that Dryden knew more of 'man in his general nature' and that the 'notions of Dryden were formed by comprehensive speculation' (*Lives*, III, 222). Dryden's 'speculation', in this case, might be included under the fourth meaning of the word as given in Johnson's *Dictionary*, 'A train of thoughts formed by meditation', but would also touch on the fifth: 'Mental scheme not reduced to practice'. Dryden's poetic thoughts, like Montaigne's in prose, appear to have been essentially itinerant – never ending, still beginning.

NOTES

1. He told Tonson in a letter dated to August 1684: 'there will be forty lines more of Virgil ... to answer those of Lucretius; I mean those very lines which Montaigne has compar'd in those two poets'. Quoted from *The Letters of John Dryden*, edited by Charles E. Ward (Durham, N.C., 1942), p. 23.

2. Several of the commentaries I have in mind are unpublished, including: Richard Bates, 'Dryden's Translations from the *Decameron*', unpublished Ph.D dissertation, University of Cambridge, 1982; Stuart Gillespie, 'Dryden's *Sylvae*', unpublished Ph.D dissertation, University of Cambridge, 1987; and John Mason, 'To Milton through Dryden and Pope', unpublished Ph.D dissertation, University of Cambridge, 1986.

3. For Lambinus, but almost certainly not for Montaigne (or for Dryden, who used the same commentary), the episode is to be read as a fable of the four elements: Mars is dry and hot, whilst Venus is moist and cold.

4. Montaigne's annotations have been transcribed and elegantly explained by M. A. Screech in *Montaigne's Annotated Copy of Lucretius* (Geneva, 1998).

5. Pierre Villey in *Les sources et l'évolution des essais de Montaigne* (Paris, 1908) records 149 quotations from Lucretius, 148 from Horace, 116 from Virgil, and 72 from Ovid.

6. *Essays of Michael Seigneur de Montaigne. With Marginal Notes, and Quotations of the cited Authors, Made English by Charles Cotton, Esq, The Third and Last Volume* (London, 1685), p. 89. All quotations from Cotton's Montaigne, including Virgil and Lucretius texts incorporated and Cotton's translations of them, are from this edition, cited as 'Cotton'.

7. *The Sixth Satire of Juvenal*, 282–3; *Poems*, III, 64.

8. John Wilson, *Specimens of the British Critics* (1846) (facsimile reprint, New York, 1979), pp. 140–2. 'Oestrum' is defined by *OED* (2a) as 'something that stings or goads one on, a stimulus; vehement impulse; passion, frenzy'.

9. *Les essais de Michel Seigneur de Montaigne* (Paris, 1598), pp. 900–1, i/j and v/u modernized, contractions expanded.

10. Lines 1–4; quoted from *The English Writings of Abraham Cowley*, edited by A. R. Waller, 2 vols (Cambridge, 1905), I, 67.

11. It may be worth observing that the phrases 'propitious queen' and 'queen of love' of the opening line were used by Waller to describe actual queens: 'propitious Queen' in 'Of the Queen', and both together in 'To the Queen'. It is almost as if Dryden is praying to the Queen of Love as the only regal power capable of such a gift: 'For thou alone that blessing canst bestow' (44). Spenser uses 'queen of love' for 'fair Venus, that is queene of loue' in *Prothalamion* (96), and for 'that sacred Saint my soueraigne Queen' in the *Faerie Queene* (IV Prologue, iv).

12. 'The Integrity of Dryden's Lucretius', *MLR*, 78 (1983), 1–23 (pp. 14–15).

13. John Mason (n. 2), pp. 31–3.

14. This is not to say that the word is inert, or Dryden's mind inactive. In his later translation of the complete *Æneid* he translated literally, rendering 'coniugis infusus gremio' as 'in her lap infused', and replacing his earlier and very different use of the word, 'all infused in joy' (*Poems*, II, 305).

15 The word 'circumfused' was available to Dryden. It was used by Ben Jonson

(but not in a sexual sense) in 'An Elegy On the Lady Jane Paulet', 69. As is pointed out by Gillespie (n. 2), p. 243, it is later used by Byron, *Childe Harold's Pilgrimage*, IV, 53: 'Glowing, and circumfused in speechless love'.

16. Norman Austin, 'Translation as Baptism: Dryden's Lucretius', *Arion*, 7 (1968), 576–602 (p. 582); Hammond (n. 12), p.17.

17. *Paradise Lost*, IV, 304–11. Here the usage would seem to resemble *OED* 3a, 'To bend, twist, or coil up into a spiral or incurved shape'. It is hair, waves, lips, smoke, mist, and flags that generally attract the epithet – or serpents, as in *Paradise Lost*: 'So varied hee, and of his tortuous Traine / Curld many a wanton wreath' (IX, 517), and as in *Alexander's Feast* when Jove, responding to the 'Power of Mighty Love' and hidden in 'a Dragon's fiery Form', rode 'Sublime on Radiant Spires' to 'fair *Olympia*', 'Then, round her slender Waste he curl'd' (Kinsley, III, 1429). Here the meaning would seem to be *OED* 6, 'To twist about, writhe'; Johnson, citing *Alexander's Feast*, glosses 'to twist itself'.

18. John Cleland, *Memoirs of a Woman of Pleasure* (London, 1749), p. 111. Elijah Fenton also noticed the word: In his version of 'Sapho to Phaon' he has Sapho recall the time 'When murm'ring in the melting Joys of Love, / Round yours my curling Limbs began to move'.

19. Lines 405–6; quoted from *The Twickenham Edition of the Poems of Alexander Pope*, VIII: *The Iliad of Homer, Books X–XXIV*, edited by Maynard Mack (London, 1967), p. 183.

20. Bates (n. 2), p. 162.

21. Bates draws attention to the lines from Dryden's version of the Third Georgic: 'The Bull's Insult at Four she may sustain; / But, after Ten, from Nuptial Rites refrain. / Six Seasons use; but then release the Cow, / *Unfit for Love*, and for the lab'ring Plough' (99–102; *Works*, III, 212; my emphasis).

'But slaves we are': Dryden and Virgil, Translation and the 'Gyant Race'

Paul Davis

This paper canvasses an unfashionable answer to a perennial question. What made translation so congenial to Dryden? Why, in the early 1680s, when he was at the height of his fame and creative powers, did he more or less abandon writing original verse, and devote the rest of his career to translating the work of other poets? No English poet of comparable stature had done this before him, and none has done it since. Critics have proposed various explanations – the current market-leaders are that 'translation offered an opportunity for oblique commentary on the times' when it might have been hazardous for Dryden, as a Roman Catholic and a Jacobite, to address political subjects openly; and that it fed his 'dramatist's fascination with the play of different voices', his 'skeptic's reluctance to adhere to any single [philosophical] system'.[1] But how might a contemporary of Dryden's have accounted for his appetite for translation? It has to be 'might', because none saw fit to express an opinion on the matter. So, imagine two observers of the Restoration literary scene sitting together in a London coffee-house some time in the late 1680s. They are discussing translation. Before too long, one or both of a pair of hallowed phrases from Horace would be brought into their discussion – 'Nec verbo verbum curabis reddere fidus / Interpres' and 'Odi imitatores servum pecus' – twin caveats against what Sir John Denham, combining them in his commendatory verses on Sir Richard Fanshawe's translation of *Il Pastor Fido* (1647), called the 'servile path ... / Of tracing word by word, and line by line'.[2] Now they turn their attention to the pre-eminent translator of the day: John Dryden. What phrases might spring to mind in connection with him? If our imaginary discutants were theatre-lovers, perhaps the first line spoken by his alter-ego Bayes in the smash hit of the previous decade, *The Rehearsal* (1671): 'Your most obsequious, and most observant, very servant, Sir.'[3] Or maybe, if poetry was more to their liking, the send-off he had received in *The Medal of John Bayes* (1682), Thomas Shadwell's recent *succès de scandale* (there might even be a copy lying around on the table to refresh their memory): 'Go *Abject Bayes*! And act thy slavish part; / Fawn on those *Popish Knaves*, whose Knave thou art.'[4] At which point, might it not occur to our putative Restoration literati to wonder whether Dryden's reputedly slavish cast of mind, and his taste for the mode of literary conduct traditionally said to bear a perilous resemblance to slavery, were linked?

To suggest as much in the present critical climate might seem recidivist, a return to the bad old days when estimates of Dryden's worth as a poet were contaminated with remnants of the *parti-pris* of his political opponents. The one contemporary of Dryden's who did insinuate such a connection was, after all, Matthew Prior, in whose early Whig session-poem 'A Satyr on the modern Translators' he appears at the 'head of [the] Gang' of 'hireling Drudges of the Age' beneath the gift-horse epigraph 'Odi imitatores servum pecus.'[5] Would it not be perverse to take the word of so hostile a witness over that of Dryden himself, who made common cause from the outset in the prefaces to his translations with the efforts of Denham, Fanshawe, and Cowley to emancipate English verse translators from the shackles of literalism, quoting approvingly in the first of them, that for the collaborative *Ovid's Epistles* (1680), Denham's praise of Fanshawe for eschewing the 'servile path'? Then again, Dryden himself would probably have acknowledged, with one of his favourite moralists, Plutarch, that 'it is the part of a Wise man, to derive Profit from his very Enemies'.[6] There are grounds for thinking that translation did indeed satisfy a desire for self-abnegation in Dryden. Prior's innuendo contains – albeit embedded within a tough husk of prejudice – a kernel of truth. In what follows I seek to dig it out.

Every student of translation theory knows that Dryden favoured the middle way of 'paraphrase, or translation with latitude' over the extremes of 'metaphrase, or turning an author word by word, and line by line', and 'imitation, where the translator ... assumes the liberty not only to vary from the words and sense, but to forsake them both as he sees occasion' (*Poems*, I, 384–5). In doing so, however, he was in part concerned to garner the polemical advantages of moderation, as appears from his deployment of the noun 'latitude', by this time the calling-card of the sweetly reasonable *via media* Anglican. If we inquire into his elaborations of that famous tripartite scheme, prying beneath their finely-gauged public demeanour into their intimate metaphorical life, we sometimes find Dryden's golden mean gravitating towards the pole of literalism, as, for instance, a little later on in the Preface to *Ovid's Epistles*:

thought, if it be translated truly, cannot be lost in another language, but the words that convey it to our apprehension (which are the image and ornament of that thought) may be so ill chosen as to make it appear in an unhandsome dress, and rob it of its native lustre. There is therefore a liberty to be allowed for the expression, neither is it necessary that words and lines should be confined to the measure of their original. The sense of an author, generally speaking, is to be sacred and inviolable. If the fancy of Ovid be luxuriant, 'tis his character to be so, and if I retrench it, he is no longer Ovid. It will be replied that he receives advantage by this lopping of his superfluous branches, but I rejoin that a translator has no such right.

(*Poems*, I, 389)

The metaphrast commits a fashion blunder, the imitator sacrilege. Conscious that to speak of the sense of an author as 'sacred and inviolable' may draw down upon him accusations of poetical fanaticism, Dryden interposes the anti-dogmatical disclaimer 'generally speaking'; but the next sentence shows that imitation and impiety were more tightly entwined in his imagination than he would have had his sect-fearing readers believe. Ovid being the poet of bodies encased in bark, to lop off his seemingly 'superfluous' branches may be to hack away not dead wood but living human limbs, to replicate the horror which Phaethon's mother Clymene perpetrates against her dendrified daughters in Book II of the *Metamorphoses*:

> She tears the bark that to each body cleaves,
> And from their verdant fingers strips away the leaves:
> The blood came trickling, where she tore away
> The leaves and bark: the maids were heard to say,
> "Forbear, mistaken parent, oh! Forbear;
> A wounded daughter in each tree you tear;"[7]

That is an early example, but repudiating the 'right[s]' of the translator was no immature tendency of Dryden's translation criticism, outgrown in later years. On the contrary, he repudiated those rights most absolutely in a passage written towards the end of his career as a translation critic, in the *Dedication of the Æneis* of 1697. He has been discussing the difficulty of matching Virgil's 'almost inexhaustible' stock of 'figurative, elegant, and sounding words':

> Besides this difficulty (with which I have strugled, and made a
> shift to pass it over) there is one remaining, which is insuperable to

all Translators. We are bound to our Author's Sense, though with the latitudes already mention'd (for I think it not so sacred, as that one Iota must not be added or diminished, on pain of an Anathema). But Slaves we are; and labour on another Man's Plantation; we dress the Vine-yard, but the Wine is the Owners: If the Soil be sometimes Barren, then we are sure of being scourg'd: If it be fruitful, and our Care succeeds, we are not thank'd; for the proud Reader will only say, the poor drudge has done his duty.

(*Works*, V, 334)

There is no more expansive account of the office – as we shall see, no other word will do – of the translator anywhere in Dryden's criticism. Signs of the special amplitude of vision in the passage include its quasi-ceremonial way with the collective pronoun, and the ritual pulse set in train by its spare parallel clauses, as well as the need Dryden evidently felt to pre-empt, at 'I think it not so sacred, as that one Iota must not be added or diminished, on pain of an Anathema', potential comparisons between its ample accents and those of the self-professed prophets whom Englishmen of his caste were in the habit of blaming for their nation's recent troubles. But it is in its metaphors that the extraordinary compass of the passage's thought most makes itself felt. To provide editorial annotation for the sentence beginning 'But slaves we are ...' would be to sketch the history of attitudes to slavery in western civilization. For that grammatical inversion retorts not merely upon the allowance of 'latitudes' which immediately precedes it, but upon the entire tradition of classical ethics which equates slavery with disgrace, the tradition from which Horace's advice to budding translators to dissociate themselves from the 'servum pecus' derives.[8] The retort is Christian in character, as is clear from the viticultural images which follow it, descendants of those used by the Old Testament prophets to describe the nation of Israel – one might compare, for instance, these verses from Deuteronomy (28: 30, 33): 'thou shalt plant a vineyard, and shalt not gather the grapes thereof ... The fruit of thy land, and all thy labours, shall a nation which thou knowest not eat up; and thou shalt be only oppressed and crushed alway' – and also from the passage's final clauses, which are informed by the parable of the unprofitable servant from Luke's Gospel (17: 7–10), as it appears in the King James Bible:

But which of you, having a servant plowing or feeding cattle, will say unto him by and by, when he is come from the field, Go and sit down to meat?
And will not rather say unto him, Make ready wherewith I may

sup, and gird thyself, and serve me till I have eaten and drunken;
and afterward thou shalt eat and drink?
Doth he thank that servant because he did the things that were
commanded him? I trow not.
So likewise ye, when ye shall have done those things which are
commanded you, say, We are unprofitable servants: we have done
that which was our duty to do.

Taken together, these two Bible readings, one from the Old
Testament, then one from the New, make up a sort of liturgy of the
word for prospective translators. To an extent they are well-matched as
a pair, a sustained reflection on the theme of servitude. Yet in combining
them Dryden favours the darker of the two possible Christian approaches
to that theme. Man enslaved himself to sin by his disobedience in the
Garden of Eden; but how is the impact of Christ's sacrifice on the
enslaved condition of sinful humanity to be construed? In some New
Testament and patristic sources it is an emancipation: from being slaves
of sin we have become sons and heirs of Christ. Had Dryden alluded to
the New Testament text which most obviously echoes and completes
Old Testament images of Israel as vineyard – the parable of the
husbandmen, in which the Israelites are destroyed and the vineyard
given to the Gentiles (Mark 12: 1–9; Luke 20: 9–16) – he would have
been endorsing that emphasis, drawing, in contemporary theological
terms, an Arminian distinction between the covenant of law which
entailed slavery, and the covenant of grace which abolishes it. But the
parable of the unprofitable servant does not sort easily with such
'covenant theology', and the exalted estimate of the capacities of human
volition which flows from it. An awkward episode 'not much discussed
in comparison with other passages' in Dryden's day, and felt by some
modern biblical scholars to be textually suspect, it has generally been
taken to show Christ denying that free will is operative in the process of
justification, and doing so with such a vengeance that, according to one
commentator, 'it is doubtful whether any other such passage can be
quoted from the New Testament in which the gratuitousness of grace is
thrown into such strong relief'.[9] By alluding to it, Dryden was promoting
the more austere understanding of the atonement associated particularly
with St Paul and St Augustine, which holds that Christ did not abolish
but reorientated the fealty of mankind, so that the beneficiaries of the
new covenant remain slaves, only slaves not of sin but of Christ.[10]
     This amounts to a hard lesson for translators. Their imaginative
subjection is aligned with the inescapable reality of man's spiritual
dependence, so that free translation becomes the poetic equivalent of the

Pelagian heresy. It might be said that this line of thought is inhibiting not only for translators but also for critics of translation. If Dryden's retort against Horace, at 'But slaves we are ...', was meant to be voiced with the spacious assurance of a profession of faith, it is doubtful whether literary critics are qualified to appraise it. Some might prefer not to, regarding Dryden's implication that the translator's loss of freedom is, like death, the wages of sin as evidence of a superstitiousness in the poet, akin to his notorious taste for astrology, which it does him little credit to revive. Even should we wish to undertake it, the task of determining the impact of so vast an intuition on the minutiae of a poet's work is a daunting one. What encourages me to believe it may be manageable in the present case is that the credal resonances of Dryden's remarks about translation in this passage of the *Dedication of the Æneis* are mediated by some literary-historical perceptions which do fall within, so to speak, the natural frequency range of literary criticism.

When Dryden said of translators that they 'labour on another man's plantation', whatever the biblical reverberations of his words, he was scoring a political point, touching a Williamite nerve. The phrase implies that translation was an especially apt activity for an English poet after 1688, since William of Orange's accession to the throne by conquest (as Jacobites and non-jurors insisted) rather than by lineal right had reduced England to the status of a Dutch colony.[11] It may even reflect specifically on the grievances of English Roman Catholics: during the Exclusion Crisis, the Roman Catholic poet John Caryll had published a political parallel comparing the threatened removal of the Duke of York from the succession to Ahab's seizure of Naboth's vineyard on trumped-up charges of disloyalty in I Kings 20-1.[12] This topical jibe is only the tip of a substantial iceberg. Its conspicuous glare alerts us to the presence of historical judgements, submerged hereabouts, which had taken Dryden's entire life of writing to form. Throughout his formative years as a poet, the vein of Old Testament images of viticulture had been mined by the hotter sorts of English protestants to fuel their rhetorics of elect nationhood, as, notably, by Marvell in *The First Anniversary of the Government under His Highness the Lord Protector* (1655):

> Thou, and thine house (like Noah's eight) did rest,
> Left by the wars' flood on the mountains' crest:
> And the large vale lay subject to thy will,
> Which thou but as an husbandman wouldst till:
> And only didst for others plant the vine
> Of liberty, not drunken with its wine.[13]

Heady hopes like those are caught up into the disabused cadence of 'But slaves we are, and labour on another Man's Plantation; we dress the Vineyard, but the Wine is the Owners' which records their disappointment, the great inversion audible now as a weary squaring-up to the fact that the English, instead of learning from the error of the ancient Israelites as Marvell had predicted, repeated it, consumed their inheritance rather than cultivating it, became 'drunken with [the] wine' of God's favour, and so, like the Israelites, forfeited it.

It would be natural to suppose that Dryden thought this catastrophic lapse had occurred somewhere during the period now known as the English Revolution, that is to say between the accession of Charles I and the final aftershocks of the Civil War in the 1670s and 1680s. In fact, however, the passage's images of dispossession reach further into the past, back to Jacobean, even Elizabethan times, and are something more than partisan, for they complete a train of thought begun in Dryden's first major work of prose, *An Essay of Dramatick Poesie* (1668), where it was his poetic heroes, 'our Fathers in Wit', Jonson, Shakespeare, and Fletcher, who had

> ruin'd their Estates themselves before they came to their childrens hands. There is scarce an Humour, a Character, or any kind of Plot, which they have not us'd. All comes sullied or wasted to us: and were they to entertain this Age, they could not now make so plenteous treatments out of such decay'd fortunes.
>
> (*Works*, XVII, 73)

Modern commentators have given various reasons for the rise of translation in late seventeenth-century England; in this passage of the *Dedication of the Æneis*, we find Dryden's. More a myth, perhaps, an *aition*, than a reason. A decade after he had been removed for his Roman Catholicism from the post of Historiographer Royal, Dryden returns to that role to frame a narrative for his nation from the rubble of its chaotic past. This narrative, at once a spiritual biography, a political history, and a literary retrospect of seventeenth-century England, has translation at its heart and as its conclusion. As William III was sent to scourge the nation for its fifty years of intoxication with political liberty, so English poets were condemned to atone for the licence of their fathers in wit by translating. For Dryden, in 1697, the servitude of translation was England's cultural destiny.

*   *   *

These thoughts about destiny and dispossession bring us close to the *Æneid*. Both Virgil's poem and Dryden's translation of it have lately been dubbed 'The Epic of Exile'.[14] But the latter at least might also be described as the epic of a neighbouring, more extreme, form of dispossession: slavery. Whereas the *Æneid* 'in contrast to the *Iliad* and the *Odyssey* has no role for a slave',[15] Dryden makes slavery seem the ineluctable condition of human life in his version of the poem by 'baldly stat[ing] that actions are "ordain'd by Fate"', as Colin Burrow has observed, 'rather than struggling to render Virgil's delicate elisions of human and divine agency'.[16] The interpolated epithet which he has Latinus apply to himself near the end of the poem – 'Slave to Fate' (*Æneis* XII, 62) – might equally serve to describe Dryden's Turnus, his Pallas, his Dido, and his Æneas. In one sense, however, the world of the *Æneid*, as Virgil presents it, is already founded on slavery – literally so, since it is held up by the forced labour of the giant Atlas. It is with Dryden's peculiar attunement to the lot of the *Æneid*'s gigantic underclass, and the relation between that attunement and his insistence in the *Dedication of the Æneis* that translators are 'slaves [who] labour on another Man's Plantation', that I shall be concerned in the second half of this paper.

Giants did not enjoy high standing – as it were – in the culture of late seventeenth-century England. The traditional interpretation of their assault on Olympus as a type of Satan's rebellion against God had been underscored by Milton's use of gigantomachic language in the War in Heaven episode of *Paradise Lost*. They were demonized in secular contexts too: Cowley used them to crown his list of the forces of superstition – '*Gods, Devils, Nymphs, Witches,* and *Giants Race*'[17] – which the new rationalist Spirit of the Age, in the form of Davenant's *Gondibert* (1651), was sweeping towards oblivion. In short, we would expect 'Virgil's recurrent use of Gigantomachic allusion to align the history of Rome and her ancestors with a cosmic conflict between the forces of chaos and Olympian order' to have made itself heard more easily to his Restoration readers than it did – until the recent work of Philip Hardie[18] – to his twentieth-century ones. A notorious feature of Dryden's handling of the scene in which giants first appear in the *Æneid* might be taken to show that he was indeed alive, only too alive, to this aspect of Virgil's epic technique: critics since the eighteenth-century classicist Joseph Trapp have objected that he coarsens the simile likening 'the Gigantomachic storm' in Book I to a plebeian mob by imputing to that mob an 'innate Desire of Blood' (*Æneis* I, 220); one modern commentator describes the moment when Triton calms the storm in Dryden's translation as an 'almost Hobbesian ... conservative celebration of order, the order of monarchy'.[19] If we look back a hundred lines or so, however, to the point at which Æolus unleashes the gigantic winds at Juno's behest, we find Dryden manifesting a measure of sympathy with them, entering into their delight at being released from long confinement with a pair of playful, Ariel-ish verbs – 'The raging Winds rush through the hollow Wound, / And dance aloft in Air, and skim along the Ground' (*Æneis* I, 122–3) – for which there is no warrant in the corresponding passage in Virgil: 'venti, velut agmine facto, / qua data porta, ruunt et terras turbine perflant' (I, 82–3: 'the winds rush out through the gap like an army drawn up for battle, and rage over the world in storm-blasts'). Nor is this anomalous in the context of the *Æneis* as a whole, for whenever giants are at issue Dryden's verse stirs to sympathetic life.

A startling instance of what one might term Dryden's 'gigantophilia' is his treatment of the hundred-headed titan Typhoeus. The most malevolent of the titans, the one whose single combat with Zeus at the end of Hesiod's *Theogony* provides the poem with its 'last climax of outrageous violence, on a cosmic scale',[20] Typhoeus' name had been further blackened in the Renaissance by allegorizers of classical epic like George Sandys, who anatomized him with grim relish as the emblem of rebellious ambition, 'having a hundred heads in regard of his divided forces; fiery mouthes, of his inflamed intents; a girdle of serpents for his pestilent malice, and seiges; iron hands, best suting with slaughter, Eagles talons, with rapin; and a body covered with feathers, in regard of perpetuall rumors, secret intelligences, fears and suspitions'.[21] He had featured in that capacity in Dryden's own *Astraea Redux*: 'Thus when the bold Typhoeus scaled the sky, / And forced great Jove from his own heaven to fly, / (What king, what crown from treason's reach is free, / If Jove and heaven can violated be?)' (37–40; *Poems*, I, 39–40). Yet somewhere between *Astraea Redux* and the *Æneis*, it seems Dryden had a change of heart about Typhoeus. He detected an uncharacteristic flicker of gigantophile sentiment in the reference Virgil makes to the arch-titan in Book IX, in connection with the collapse of a rock-tower near Arima, the earthquake-prone region where he was traditionally said to have been imprisoned: 'durumque cubile / inarime Iovis armipotens imposta Typhoeo' (715–16: 'Jove laid Arima over Typhoeus – a hard bed'). Given that inch, Dryden took this mile:

> *Typhoeus* thrown beneath, by *Jove*'s Command,
> Astonish'd at the Flaw, that shakes the Land,
> Soon shifts his weary Side, and scarce awake,
> With Wonder feels the weight press lighter on his Back.
>   (*Æneis* IX, 969–72; *Works*, VI, 671–2)

These two couplets are a gem after Virgil's 'subjective style'.[22] Dryden gives Typhoeus a breather from his eternity on the receiving end: by raising him from grammatical subordination in the ablative absolute 'imposta Typhoeo' to the head of the sentence, and in particular by 'focalizing' the lines through his point of view. The giant's relief at being able to uncoil his eternally cramped limbs sounds in the stretch of half-rhymes and alliterations 'awake, / ... Wonder ... weight ... lighter', which revel in the freedom for manoeuvre they find within their limited acoustic space; and then too in the passage's ending on an alexandrine, the syllabic equivalent of an increase in leg-room. Preferring the decasyllabic over the octosyllabic couplet for translating Juvenal in the 'Discourse concerning the Original and Progress of Satire', Dryden gave as his reason that 'this sort of number is more roomy. The thought can turn itself with greater ease in a larger compass' (*Poems*, III, 439).

It's an extraordinary moment, ahead of its time. To find an analogue for it, we must cast our minds forward to the Romantics, to *Hyperion* perhaps, where Keats compassionates 'Typhon' and his brother-titans 'pent in regions of laborious breath; / Dungeoned in opaque element ... / Without a motion, save of their big hearts / Heaving in pain'.[23] Lest it be thought merely quirky, let's pursue Dryden's gigantophile tendencies a little further where they lead. Which is deep into the symbolic core of the *Æneid*, towards the Shield of Æneas, the 'cosmic emblem ... fitly placed at the end of the central, prospective and prophetic books' of the poem.[24] The shield is the work of the Cyclopes, whom Vulcan commissions to forge it when he descends into the bowels of Etna two-thirds of the way through Book VIII:

> On their Eternal Anvils here he found
> The Brethren beating, and the Blows go round:
> A load of pointless Thunder now there lies
> Before their Hands, to ripen for the Skies:
> These Darts, for angry *Jove*, they dayly cast:
> Consum'd on Mortals with prodigious waste.
> (*Æneis* VIII, 561–6; *Works*, VI, 625)

Here again, Dryden focalizes the scene from the giants' perspective. Consider first 'A load of pointless thunder'. In Virgil, the Cyclopes have only one unfinished thunderbolt at hand when Vulcan arrives, which Dryden's phrase not only multiplies but also invests with a sweeping power of metaphorical suggestion undreamt of in Virgil's sober 'pars imperfecta manebat' ('part of it remained to be completed').[25] For 'load' in Dryden's poems regularly solicits 'life', general contemplation of the burden of being, as in *Lucretius: Against the Fear of Death* when Nature advises 'If life be grown a load, a real ill, / And I would all thy cares and labours end, / Lay down thy burden, fool, and know thy friend' (135–7; *Poems*, II, 323); in *The Tenth Satire of Juvenal* which similarly recommends cultivation of 'A soul that can securely death defy, / And count it nature's privilege to die; / Serene and manly, hardened to sustain / The load of life, and exercised in pain' (550–3; *Poems*, III, 131); and in the second book of *Palamon and Arcite* where Palamon declares 'Our Life's a Load; encumber'd with the Charge, / We long to set th' imprisoned Soul at large' (265–6; Kinsley, IV, 1490).²⁶ 'Pointless' confirms that Dryden intended the unfinished thunderbolts to function as an emblem of the load of the Cyclopes' servile lives: 'pointless' as in 'blunt', of course, but also 'undirected' (the Cyclopes do not get a say in where their thunderbolts are aimed), and therefore 'meaningless' (the proletariat of the cosmos, they are deprived of the chance to invest their lives with meaning through their labour), but nevertheless 'never-ending' (they labour at 'Eternal Anvils'). This aggrieved fellow-feeling continues into the penultimate line, at 'they dayly cast', which stirs thoughts of what might have been, a world in which the Cyclopes could cast – throw – their thunderbolts for themselves, instead of having to cast – forge – them to be thrown by Jupiter. And it comes to a head in the final line, at 'with prodigious waste', a piece of 'free indirect style', Dryden's draft of an appeal on behalf of the monstrous blacksmiths: 'if threatening to lay the world waste cost us our freedom, why, when 'Jove' does the same thing, is it called justice?' Or, simply, 'And He calls us monsters!'

That Dryden should have commiserated with the Cyclopes is more remarkable than his having done so with the gigantic winds or even with Typhoeus. For the ancient gigantomachies make a crucial distinction between the Cyclopes and the rest of the 'Giant Race'. In the 'debate / Of empire', as Dryden put it in his *First Book of Ovid's Metamorphoses*, 'when our universal state / Was put to hazard', the Cyclopes fought on the side of the Olympian gods.²⁷ They forged the thunderbolts which Zeus used to defeat their titan-brothers. So, if slaving away at Vulcan's anvils was a 'waste' of the Cyclopes' 'prodigious' powers, it was servitude they had chosen for themselves. When Dryden pleads the case for their emancipation, he is putting words into their mouths which they would have disowned. As well as being misplaced, his sympathies are spectacularly mistimed. As Philip Hardie points out, in Virgil this scene is counterpointed against the episode in Book I when Juno visits Æolus to enlist his aid in her cause: 'The caves of Æolus and of the Cyclopes are both presented as centres of immense elemental power' – but 'with the essential difference that in the first that power is used irresponsibly,

whereas in the second it is the instrument of a divine providence.'
Dryden's protest that the Cyclopes have been reduced to the status of
instruments coincides with their being revealed as instrumental to the
fabric of the Virgilian universe, their beginning work on the Shield of
Æneas, which symbolizes that universe.[28]

His own phrase 'A load of pointless thunder', which epitomizes his
sympathy for the Cyclopes, betrays the radically anti-Virgilian nature of
that sympathy. First, in that identifying their predicament as one of
loadedness summons the quintessential image of the quintessential
Virgilian value, *pietas*: Æneas, 'loaded' with his father Anchises (*Æneis*
II, 1093, 963), making his way out of the wreck of Troy.[29] Then, in that
Dryden considered pointlessness a virtue in an epic poet, and thought no
epic poet more pointless than Virgil. His critical essays are thick with
passages depreciating epic poets who succumb to the temptation of
'points, and ... somewhat which had more of the sting of an epigram,
than of the dignity and state of an Heroick Poem' (of Lucan; *Works*, XI,
11), 'conceits, points of epigram, and witticisms; all which are not only
below the dignity of heroic verse, but contrary to its nature' (of Tasso;
Poems III, 332), by comparison with Virgil who is 'everywhere above
conceits of epigrammatic wit and gross hyperboles ... maintains majesty
in the midst of plainness ... shines but glares not' (*Poems*, II, 242). If
Virgil's Cyclopes have something of a poetic air about them, plying their
hammers 'in numerum' (VIII, 453; 'in measured cadence'), Dryden's,
labouring pointlessly, are proto-Virgilian epicists, gigantic avatars of
Virgil who, like them, eschewed the hurling of pointed barbs, though he
'could have written sharper satires than either Horace or Juvenal, if he
would have employed his talent that way' (*Poems*, III, 414).

The word Dryden used to commemorate Virgil's deliberated
pointlessness, the poesies he nipped in the bud, was 'retrenchment'. A
celebrated passage in the *Dedication of the Æneis* eulogizes his 'Manners,
his judicious management of the Figures, the sober retrenchments of his
Sense, which always leaves somewhat to gratifie our imagination, on
which it may enlarge at pleasure' (*Works*, V, 326). To 'retrench', in
horticulture, is to pare away exuberant blooms in the interests of long-
term growth, to prune, so that, under the terms of Dryden's theory
about England's poetic past, Virgil's Cyclopean habit of 'retrenchment'
constitutes the necessary corrective to the imaginative profligacy of the
Elizabethans and Jacobeans. It is the habit which the poets of Dryden's
generation needed to cultivate above any other, if they were to succeed
in replanting the estates 'ruin'd' by their 'Fathers in Wit', re-dressing
the vineyard which their sires had drunk dry. Yet, when Dryden
encountered such 'retrenchment' in practice, in the cave of the Cyclopes,

he could see no merit in the 'prodigious waste' of powers it entailed; looking on the Cyclopes as titanic Uncle Toms, he as good as goaded them to show some solidarity with their giant-brothers, to rise up against their Olympian oppressors. His contemporaries may have referred to him as 'the English Virgil', but it appears Dryden was too much of a gigantophile to be the kind of Virgil he insisted his age required.

Samuel Johnson could have told him as much:

> Next to argument, his delight was in wild and daring sallies of sentiment, in the irregular and excentrick violence of wit. He delighted to tread upon the brink of meaning, where light and darkness begin to mingle; to approach the precipice of absurdity, and hover over the abyss of unideal vacancy.[30]

Would Dryden have conceded the justice of these analogies between his poetic temperament and the gigantic 'forces of nature, whose uprising threatens not only the hegemony of the Olympian gods but also the structure of the physical universe' in the *Æneid*?[31] Would he have acknowledged that gigantism was latent in him, that thing of darkness his? Perhaps. A few years before he turned his attention to translating Virgil, he had likened himself in the opening lines of the Prologue to *Amphitryon* (1690) to a 'lab'ring Bee' who

> when his sharp sting is gone,
> Forgets his Golden Work, and turns a drone:
> Such is a satyr, when you take away
> That rage, in which his noble vigour lay.
>   (1–4; *Poems*, IV, 235)

The metaphor has Cyclopean undertones. Virgil compares the industry of bees to that of the Cyclopes in Book IV of the *Georgics* (170–8; Dryden's 245–57 in *Works*, V, 247); and, as we have seen, the Cyclopes' willingness to have their stings drawn by the Olympian gods figures the 'pointless' poetics of the *Æneid*. Bridling at the loss of his poetic 'sting' in these lines, Dryden may already have suspected that he was not the poet to undertake on behalf of his culture the labours of 'retrenchment' Virgil performed for Augustan Rome. Ten years later, in the Preface to *Fables*, he made a more open admission of the misfit between his poetic constitution and that of Virgil: 'I have found by Trial, *Homer* a more pleasing Task than *Virgil* ... For the *Grecian* is more according to my Genius, than the *Latin* Poet', elaborating his preference for Homer in terms which imply recognition of the gigantic features of his own 'distinguishing character' as a poet: '*Virgil* was of a quiet, sedate Temper; *Homer* was violent, impetuous, and full of Fire' (Kinsley, IV, 1448). But the most telling indications that Dryden knew he was one of the giants of English poetry, that the 'boist'rous ... wit' of that 'giant race' had not been altogether 'tamed ... to manners' in the Restoration, as is tidily supposed in 'To My Dear Friend Mr Congreve, On His Comedy called *The Double-Dealer*' (5–10; *Poems*, IV, 328–9), are to be found elsewhere. In the observation in the *Dedication of the Æneis* that "tis one thing to take pains on a Fragment, and Translate it perfectly; and another thing to have the weight of a whole Author on my shoulders' (*Works*, V, 325–6), his Virgilian labours are connected not only with Æneas' carrying of Anchises but also with the duty of sustaining the earth which Jupiter inflicted on Atlas.[32] And there is the passage with which I began this paper:

> But Slaves we are; and labour on another Man's Plantation; we dress the Vine-yard, but the Wine is the Owners: If the Soil be sometimes Barren, then we are sure of being scourg'd: If it be fruitful, and our Care succeeds, we are not thank'd; for the proud Reader will only say, the poor drudge has done his duty.

This is the sort of thing the Cyclopes might have said in reply to Dryden's accusation that they were demeaning themselves by 'ripen[ing]' their thunderbolts for Jupiter's benefit rather than their own ends. They might have grumbled that they were 'poor drudge[s]', perhaps also that they were 'not thanked' for the services they rendered their Olympian masters, even that those Olympian masters were 'proud'; but sooner or later they would have reminded Dryden of the plain fact that the gods and not they were the 'owner[s]' of the world, and, with that, returned to their anvils. The idea that translating is like standing on the shoulders of giants is a familiar one; here Dryden imagines translators themselves as docile giants, who, like the Cyclopes, embrace enslavement to prevent their gigantic powers from laying the world to 'prodigious waste'. The immoveable quality of the inversion 'But slaves we are', and the clenched parallelisms of the succeeding clauses, suggest the depth of Dryden's personal attachment to this view of the translator, how much he needed to believe that translating would domesticate his gigantic instincts.

We may be glad that, in the event, it didn't; that in the poetic practice of the *Æneis* as opposed to the theorizing of the *Dedication*, Dryden proved to be too big for the Cyclopes' boots. For the liberties he took with Virgil's text wherever giants are concerned give rise to some of the finest passages of the translation. Then too, speaking more generally, had

Dryden succeeded in excising from his work every trace of his gigantic traits, he would have turned out a lesser poet, the sort of relentlessly decorous 'Augustan' he was taken to be throughout much of the nineteenth and twentieth centuries. Some of the best recent work on his verse emphasizes that it is often 'violent, impetuous, and full of Fire', as he said Homer's was;[33] and recovering this 'Homeric' side of him may help to win him a new generation of readers. Nevertheless, we should not brush aside his own anxieties about what he would have termed the 'strength' of his poems as so much neurosis or superstition. Dryden would not have been sheerly delighted to have the gigantophile leanings of the *Æneis* brought to his attention by a reader; if we are, we substitute for 'his three-dimensional response' to 'the differing aspects and values of strength' the 'one-sided enthusiasm for all things strong' to which, as Eric Griffiths warns, 'modern literary history often ... tends'.[34] That tendency stems in part from the fact that the giants have become dead metaphors, so that a tale such as that of the Pierids in Book V of Ovid's *Metamorphoses* – in which the nine daughters of Pierius challenge the Muses to a poetry contest, and, taking gigantomachy as the subject of their poem, are punished with the loss of their human form 'for their arrogance and impudence; but above all for extolling the flagitious giants'[35] – now seems the merest whimsy. But for Dryden it was no flight of fancy back to a time in his nation's recent past when the 'State / Was put to hazard' by the 'arrogance and impudence' of a 'Gyant Race'. One might say that Dryden feared English poets were genetically predisposed towards gigantism, that chaotic 'strength' was in his DNA. A part of him hoped to screen his culture against it by translating.

NOTES

1. Paul Hammond, 'Classical Texts: Translations and Transformations', in *The Cambridge Companion to English Literature, 1650–1740*, edited by Steven Zwicker (Cambridge, 1998), pp. 143–61 (p. 148). Professor Hammond's own work has been instrumental in the development of the latter of these approaches: see in particular his 'John Dryden: The Classicist as Sceptic', *The Seventeenth Century*, 4 (1989), 165–87. The former approach, outlined by Steven Zwicker, *Politics and Language in Dryden's Poetry* (Princeton, 1984), pp. 177–205, has been best exemplified recently by Howard Erskine-Hill, *Poetry and the Realm of Politics: Shakespeare to Dryden* (Oxford, 1996), pp. 201–15.

2. 'To Sir *Richard Fanshaw* upon His Translation of *Pastor Fido*', 15–16. Horace's warnings, which appear in the *Ars poetica* and *Epistles* I.xix respectively, were in fact meant for prospective imitators, not translators, but their influence over seventeenth-century discussions of poetic translation can scarcely be overstated.

3. *The Rehearsal*, edited by D. E. L. Crane (Durham, 1976), I.i.50.

4. *The Medal of John Bayes*, reprinted in *John Dryden: The Critical Heritage*, edited by James and Helen Kinsley (London, 1971), pp. 143–50 (p. 149).

5. 'A Satyr on the modern Translators' (1685), 23, 2; quoted from *The Literary Works of Matthew Prior*, edited by H. Bunker Wright and Monroe K. Spears, 2 vols (Oxford, 1959), I, 19.

6. Henry Vaughan, 'Of the Benefit we may get by our Enemies' (1651), in *The Works of Henry Vaughan*, edited by L. C. Martin (1914; reprint Oxford, 1957), p. 97. The sentiment was something of a commonplace among the ancients: Plutarch is quoting Xenophon.

7. Quoted from the translation of the episode by Joseph Addison, reprinted in Samuel Garth's composite English *Metamorphoses* (1717), edited by Garth Tissol (Ware, 1998), p. 49.

8. A crisp survey of this tradition, supported by sample quotation from the major source-texts, may be found in Peter Garnsey, *Ideas of Slavery from Aristotle to Augustine* (Cambridge, 1996), pp. 105–52.

9. Ross Garner, *The Unprofitable Servant in Henry Vaughan* (Lincoln, NE, 1963), p. 41; C. F. Evans, *Saint Luke* (London, 1990), pp. 619–21; Ronald Knox, *A New Testament Commentary for English Readers*, Vol. 1: *The Gospels* (London, 1953), p. 170.

10. For further discrimination of these two emphases within the Christian understanding of slavery, see Garnsey, pp. 220–35.

11. Two examples of this anti-Williamite analysis are Jeremy Collier, *Dr Sherlock's Case of Allegiance Consider'd* (1691), and John Kettlewell, *The Duty of Allegiance Settled upon its True Grounds* (1691). For a narrative of the controversy over the grounds of William's authority, see J. P. Kenyon, *Revolution Principles* (Cambridge, 1977), pp. 24–9.

12. John Caryll, *Naboth's Vineyard* (1679), in *Anthology of Poems on Affairs of State: Augustan Satirical Verse, 1660–1714*, edited by George deForest Lord (New Haven, 1975), pp. 205–18.

13. *The First Anniversary of the Government under His Highness the Lord Protector*, 283–8, quoted from *Andrew Marvell*, edited by Frank Kermode and Keith Walker (Oxford, 1990), p. 99.

14. By, respectively, Philip Hardie, in his superb *Virgil* (Oxford, 1998), p. 66, and Paul Hammond, who adopts the phrase as the subtitle of his chapter on the *Æneis* in *Dryden and the Traces of Classical Rome* (Oxford, 1999).

15. Richard Jenkyns, *Virgil's Experience* (Oxford, 1998), p. 16.

16. Colin Burrow, 'Virgil in English Translation', in *The Cambridge Companion to Virgil*, edited by Charles Martindale (Cambridge, 1997), pp. 21–37 (p. 29).

17. 'To Sir William Davenant, Upon his two first Books of *Gondibert*, finished before his voyage to America' (1650), in *Gondibert*, edited by David F. Gladish (Oxford, 1971), pp. 270–1.

18. The phrase I quote is from his *Virgil* (p. 94), but for the full elaboration of his provocative thesis, see *Virgil's Æneid: Cosmos and Imperium* (Oxford, 1986).

19. T. W. Harrison, 'Dryden's *Aeneid*', in *Dryden's Mind and Art*, edited by Bruce King (Edinburgh, 1969), pp. 143–67 (p. 167); Harrison's remarks are founded on Trapp's objection to the politics of the scene in Dryden as 'too

gross and horrid for Virgil's meaning'. The gigantomachic resonances of the storm are detailed in Hardie, *Virgil's Aeneid*, pp. 90–7.

20. Robert Lamberton, *Hesiod* (New Haven, 1988), p. 89.

21. Sandys, *Ovid's Metamorphoses Englished* (1632; facsimile reprint New York, 1976), pp. 190–1. Milton used Typhoeus as a mythological double for Satan both in his early allegory of the Gunpowder Plot, 'In Quintum Novembris', and in *Paradise Lost*.

22. The properties of this style were originally outlined in Brooks Otis, *Virgil: A Study in Civilised Poetry* (Oxford, 1964), Ch. 3; some of today's Virgilians prefer to use the term 'focalization' (which I adopt below), coined by the French narratologist Gerard Genette (see *Narrative Discourse*, translated by Jane Lewin (Ithaca, 1980), pp. 189–94), as, for instance, in D. P. Fowler, 'Deviant focalisation in Virgil's *Aeneid*', *Proceedings of the Cambridge Philological Society*, 36 (1990), 42–63.

23. *Hyperion*, II, 20–7, quoted from *The Poems of John Keats*, edited by Miriam Allott (Harlow, 1970), pp. 417–18.

24. Hardie, *Virgil's Aeneid*, p. 362.

25. Dryden's suggestive rendering of the phrase may owe something to the application of the adjective 'inchoatum' to the unfinished thunderbolt in the prose *interpretatio* in the edition of Virgil on which he mainly relied, that of Ruaeus. See *Publii Vergilii Maronis Opera* (Amsterdam, 1690), p. 653.

26. For additional instances in the Dryden corpus, see *Iphis and Ianthe*, 28; *Æneis* XII, 781; and *Cinyras and Myrrha*, 368.

27. Lines 237–8; *Poems*, IV, 243. See Hesiod, *Theogony*, edited by M. L. West (Oxford, 1966), 139–53, 140, 142, 501; and for instances of this distinction in other titanomachies, Stella Purce Revard, *The War in Heaven* (Ithaca, 1980), pp. 149–50 (n. 45).

28. Hardie, *Virgil's Aeneid*, pp. 105, 336–7.

29. The centrality of *pietas* in Dryden's understanding of the *Æneid* appears, for instance, in his endorsement of Segrais's defence of Virgil for 'giving the preference to Piety before Valour', and making that piety 'the first Character of *Æneas*' (*Dedication of the Æneis*, *Works*, V, 288, 295).

30. 'Life of Dryden', in *Lives*, I, 460. The classic exposition of this passage in relation to Dryden's poetic tastes is Harold Love, 'Dryden's "Unideal Vacancy"', *Eighteenth-Century Studies*, 12 (1978), 74–89.

31. Hardie, *Virgil's Aeneid*, p. 95. He is referring to the gigantic storm in Book I, which offers many instances of the mingling of antithetical elements Johnson describes – opportunities in which Dryden's translation revels, as at 'sable Night involves the Skies; / And Heav'n it self is ravish'd from their Eyes' (*Æneis* I, 129–30).

32. This is a natural extrapolation, given that Æneas' shouldering of Anchises is invested with 'Atlantean' nuance by Virgil, as is his later shouldering of the shield at the end of Book VIII: for detail and discussion, see Hardie, *Virgil's Aeneid*, pp. 372–3.

33. See in particular Eric Griffiths, 'Dryden's Past', *PBA*, 84 (1994), 113–49 (pp. 127–31); Robin Sowerby, 'The Freedom of Dryden's Homer', *Translation and Literature*, 5 (1996), 26–50; and Hammond, *Dryden and the Traces of Classical Rome* (n. 14), pp. 209–10.

34. Griffiths, p. 141.
35. *Metamorphoses*, V, 662–78; for this interpretation of the story, see Sandys, *Metamorphoses* (n. 21), pp. 190–1, 199 (from which I quote). The challenging idea suggested by Stephen Hinds that Ovid intended the Pierids to be seen not only as 'impious' but also as epitomes of outmoded poetic taste would have enhanced any tendency in Dryden to identify with them, given his habit of describing himself as the 'hindmost of the last' poetic age ('Prologue to *Aureng-Zebe*', 22, *Poems*, I, 298; Hinds, *The Metamorphosis of Persephone* (Cambridge, 1987), pp. 127–33).

Dryden at his Tercentenary

Paul Davis

John Dryden: Tercentenary Essays, edited by Paul Hammond and David Hopkins. Pp. 432. Oxford: Clarendon Press, 2000. Hb. £65.

The publishers of *John Dryden: Tercentenary Essays* are to be congratulated for making it so beautiful a book to handle and to open; and its editors for, among other things, handling its opening so beautifully. On the title page, a simple dedication 'To the Memory of John Dryden, 1631–1700' is set off by an epigraph below:

> *The Soul returns to Heav'n, from whence it came;*
> *Earth keeps the Body, Verse preserves the Fame.*

Plain enough, one might think – until one remembers what Dryden himself made of 'To the Memory of ... ', his uncommon way with that common memorial, in 'To the Memory of Mr Oldham' (1684), one of the few of his poems to hold its place in anthologies throughout the period of his critical neglect which this volume seeks to bring to an end. Remembering this much, one might think it rash of the editors to court comparison between their memorial for Dryden and Dryden's masterpiece of commemoration – until one further notices that the couplet which completes the dedication is taken from 'To my Honour'd Kinsman John Driden' (1700), the poem which Dryden described in a letter to the Whig poet and politician Charles Montagu as 'a Memorial of my own Principles to all Posterity'. Seventeenth-century funeral elegists commonly observed that the death of the person whose memorial they were writing had deprived the world of the one person properly qualified to write that memorial, so that it suggests not only the depth of Paul Hammond's and David Hopkins's loyalty to Dryden, but also the breadth of their acquaintance with the circumstances in which he worked, that this volume of commemorative essays begins by commemorating its subject's own eminence in the literary arts of commemoration.

Dryden himself chose William Congreve to commemorate his memory, exhorting the young playwright to 'Be kind to my remains' in the commendatory poem he provided for Congreve's first play *The Double-*

Dealer in 1693, seven years before his death. Congreve fulfilled that obligation twenty-four years later, in the Epistle Dedicatory of *The Dramatick Works of John Dryden, Esq: in Six Volumes* (1717); and the terms of his memorial for his departed friend and mentor have been invoked again and again in recent times by commentators – prominent among them both Professor Hammond and Dr Hopkins – set on countering the unfavourable impression of Dryden bequeathed to modern readers by his political and poetical adversaries. Congreve particularly recalled Dryden's generosity to other writers, generosity from which – as is demonstrated afresh here by Jennifer Brady's discussion of 'Dryden and Congreve's Collaboration in *The Double Dealer*' – he himself had handsomely benefited:

> [Dryden] was not more possess'd of Knowledge than he was Communicative of it. But then his Communication of it was by no means pedantick, or impos'd upon the Conversation; but just such, and went so far as by the natural Turns of the Discourse in which he was engag'd it was necessarily promoted or required.

This generosity Dryden exercised not only towards his contemporaries during his lifetime, but also towards his poetic descendants after his death, in which extended sense it is commemorated here by Tom Mason and Adam Rounce, whose essay '*Alexander's Feast; Or The Power of Musique*: The Poem and Its Readers' takes pains to record the many cases in which Dryden's great ode communicated to eighteenth- and nineteenth-century poets just such 'a fragment of an image, ... prompting towards a general thought' or 'hint of harmony' as was required by the natural turns of the discourse upon which they were engaged. As well as commemorating Dryden's generous communicative-ness, this volume may be said to imitate it, for its two longest chapters – John Barnard's 'Dryden, Tonson, and the Patrons of *The Works of Virgil* (1697)', which culminates in a table of the 349 subscribers to the Virgil organized by title, profession, politics, age, and education; and Paul Hammond's Appendix listing in chronological order seventy-four 'Contemporary References to Dryden', many of them from manuscript sources and most hitherto unknown – amount to a rich heirloom for Dryden scholarship, a fund of knowledge arduously gleaned but freely handed on to future admirers of the poet.

The *John Dryden* these *Tercentenary Essays* primarily commend to our memory is John Dryden the translator. Whilst only two of the thirteen – Robin Sowerby's study of Dryden's version of 'The Last Parting of Hector and Andromaque', and James Winn's '"According to my Genius":

Dryden's Translation of "The First Book of Homer's *Ilias*'" – examine, at a nuts-and-bolts level, how Dryden went about the practical business of rendering classical poetry into English, another four – Paul Hammond's introductory 'Is Dryden a Classic?', Cedric Reverand II's 'The Final "Memorial of My Own Principles": Dryden's Alter Egos in His Later Career', and Steven Zwicker's 'Dryden and the Dissolution of Things: The Decay of Structures in Dryden's Later Writing', along with Professor Barnard's piece on the subscribers to the *Virgil* – base their arguments exclusively or preponderantly on examples drawn from Dryden's translations. Of the remaining seven, a further three – Howard Erskine-Hill's 'MacFlecknoe, Heir of Augustus', Nicholas von Maltzahn's 'Dryden's Milton and the Theatre of the Imagination', and David Hopkins's 'Editing, Authenticity, and Translation: Re-Presenting Dryden's Poetry in 2000' – might be thought to be, or think of themselves as being, about 'translation' in some derived or metaphorical sense of the word. The first, teasing out the connections between Dryden's mock-enthronement of Thomas Shadwell and the pageantry which accompanied the coronation of Charles II, offers *Mac Flecknoe* as an instance of what Paul Hammond, introducing the volume, terms the 'inventive way in which the literary, political, and religious issues of his day' are in Dryden's original writings 'translated into poetry, mythologized, and brought into contact with classical culture'; the second fascinatingly exposes the libertine manuscript pre-history of *The State of Innocence* (1677), Dryden's '"translation" of Milton's epic'; and the third explores 'parallels ... between Dryden's own activity as a translator and an editor's activity in modernizing and annotating Dryden's work for a modern reader'.

In finding Dryden's translations his most memorable works, while for the most part practising what his friend, the playwright and sometime ambassador George Etherege called 'the exquisite art of forgetfulness' in respect of the drama – represented only by Paulina Kewes's 'Dryden and the Staging of Popular Politics' – and even the political poems and early critical essays on which his reputation used to rest (neither *Absalom and Achitophel* nor *An Essay of Dramatick Poesie* is treated at length), *John Dryden: Tercentenary Essays* confirms a reorientation of critical priorities observable in many recent studies of the poet, particularly those written on this side of the Atlantic. We might – I certainly do – welcome that development, and yet feel that, by defining 'translation' more and more inclusively, this volume takes it to new and not unproblematic lengths. Once one can speak of the process by which Dryden shaped 'quotidian experience into fictive form' as 'translating', as Paul Hammond does here, or argue, with David Hopkins, that 'the complex dialogue between present and past' in which 'the process of reading an older literary text' in one's own mother tongue takes place amounts to 'translation', so that whenever Dryden picked up a volume of Jonson, Shakespeare, or Cowley he was in a sense 'translating', not only does every one of Dryden's works qualify as 'translation', but so too would the entire corpus of every poet before or after him, except those (imaginary, or else unreadable) few who combine a surreal extremity of vision with an absolute lack of interest in the achievements of their predecessors.

Dryden himself sometimes treated the idea of 'translation' in an expansive manner, as, notably, in the lines from 'Of the Pythagorean Philosophy; From Ovid's *Metamorphoses* Book XV' which provide the starting-point for Charles Tomlinson's fine account of his versions of Ovid in *Poetry and Metamorphosis*:

> Those very Elements which we partake
> Alive, when dead some other Bodies make:
> Translated grow, have Sense, or can Discourse;
> But Death on deathless Substance has no Force.

But he was also aware that to do so was to risk evacuating the term of meaning, as when he commented in the Preface to *Ovid's Epistles* that in 'imitation', as practised by Cowley, 'the translator (if now he has not lost that name) assumes the liberty not only to vary from the words and sense, but to forsake them both as he sees occasion'. Subsuming as much of Dryden's work under the name of 'translation' as this volume invites us to may have the effect not of heightening the profile of translation within Dryden's career – as Hammond and Hopkins presumably and laudably intended – but of diluting awareness of the unique extent of Dryden's commitment to the distinctive task of rendering poems from one language into another. To assess translations, as opposed to 'translations', critics need special tools, the precise linguistic acumen brought to bear in this volume particularly by Robin Sowerby, in his close reading of 'The Last Parting of Hector and Andromaque', and which has distinguished the work of Hammond and Hopkins throughout their many years of writing about – and now editing – Dryden's translations. The individual character of these practical skills needs to be reaffirmed in the present circumstances, when fewer and fewer commentators trouble to acquire them, opting instead for the looser, less hard-won theoretical competences which are supposed uniformly adequate now that, as the deconstructionist mantra goes, 'All writing is translation.'

One form of writing Dryden did associate with translation was the writing of memorials, a fact which – together with the special pride and pleasure he takes in his translations in various of his letters and critical essays – makes it peculiarly appropriate that he should be memorialized as a translator. The association is most apparent in *Fables Ancient and Modern*. Comprised for the most part of translations, from Homer, Ovid, Chaucer, and Boccaccio, the few original pieces it contains are memorials, or can be thought of as such: 'To Her Grace the Dutchess of Ormond', the panegyric which opens the volume, is as concerned to honour the memory of her ancestors as it is to praise the Duchess herself (an emphasis already apparent in the prose Dedication to her husband which precedes it); 'To my Honour'd Kinsman, John Driden' represents, as we have seen, Dryden's 'memorial' to his 'own principles', a memorial to which 'The Character of a Good Parson', 'Imitated from Chaucer' but substantially 'inlarg'd', forms a spiritual coda; and then there is 'The Monument of A Fair Maiden Lady, Who dy'd at Bath, and is there Interr'd', the last and least-remembered of the volume's acts of remembrance. The imaginative kinship which underlies this physical conjunction is brought out in the Preface by Dryden's moving, musing response to the news that Mademoiselle de Scudéry had begun to translate Chaucer into French at about the same time as he was himself engaged in modernizing a selection of the *Canterbury Tales*: 'it makes me think; that there is something in it like Fatality; that after certain Periods of Time, the Fame and Memory of Great Wits should be renew'd, as *Chaucer* is both in *France* and *England*'.

Dryden's having included a number of commemorative poems beneath the rubric of *Fables Ancient and Modern* may be taken to imply his consciousness of the fictive dimension of memorial writing. That dimension of the memorials which the poet composed for himself – how he contrived, for instance, 'to negotiate the real disparities between himself and the other John Driden into a concord' – is ably explored in Cedric Reverand's essay on 'Dryden's Alter Egos'. But what of the memorial these *Tercentenary Essays* compose for him? How much of the *John Dryden* whose 'Fame and Memory' they 'renew' three hundred years after his death is fictional? Considering the related question which confronts a modern editor of Dryden – how much of the authentic meaning and impact of his poems is lost if their accidentals are modernized for the convenience of twenty-first century readers? – Hopkins asserts that, while an editor 'preparing a modernized edition of Dryden's works' must be 'constantly aware that he ... is dealing with a document from a world ... quite different from his own', 'such an edition acknowledges that the only viable life that a literary text can have is in the re-creating imaginations of readers in the present'. And he

offers as a model of such responsible modernizing practice Dryden's
dealings with Chaucer, who is 'entirely rethought and represented in a
modern idiom' in *Fables*, but originals of whose texts were also reprinted
at the back of Dryden's volume, so that its readers 'were constantly
encouraged to give equal weight to the alteration and continuity of words
and things, to the cultural and linguistic conditions which joined, and
those which separated, them from Chaucer'. One might equally adduce
Dryden's handling of Homer, where he aimed to achieve a similar
balance within the translations themselves, as Robin Sowerby and James
Winn show in their twin studies, directing us to his employment of
archaic diction and metrical effects as a counterweight to his rethinking
of Homeric idiom.

A consciously archaizing style is plainly not the same as an archaic one.
Since archaism had specific cultural meanings in seventeenth-century
poetic culture, after *The Shepheards Calendar* and *Hamlet*, readers of
Dryden's Homer were not encountering the Greek poet in the
primitivizing features of his Homeric verse, any more than, as Hopkins
points out, performances of Baroque music on authentic instruments,
and by analogy old-spelling editions of Renaissance poets, provide
modern listeners with 'a uniquely authentic record of their authors'
intentions'. But this does not mean that performing Bach on authentic
instruments in front of twenty-first century audiences, or for that matter
reprinting 'original' texts of Chaucer for Restoration readers, serves no
purpose; rather, that the purpose it serves is not that of securing the holy
grail of 'authenticity', but the more practicable one of presenting, in the
words of a critic of the early music movement approvingly quoted by
Hopkins, '[a] defamiliarising challenge ... to modern ... expectations'.
So, to return to the question of how much of the Dryden commemorated
in these *Tercentenary Essays* is a fictional creation, we might perhaps
rephrase it by asking whether the Dryden who is 'rethought' and 'represented' in this volume presents a sufficiently defamiliarizing challenge
to modern expectations, to current critical priorities.

On this score I have my doubts. One reason why Dryden's translations
of Chaucer do something more than trick out 'a dry, old-fashioned wit'
as a fashionable poet whom sophisticated Restoration readers would
think 'worth receiving', and would deign to be at home to, is that
Dryden was not altogether sure what drew him to translate Chaucer in
the first place, finding only, as we have seen, 'something in it like
Fatality' that the author of *The Canterbury Tales* should have been
'renew'd' at the turn of the eighteenth century. Had Dryden translated
Chaucer out of a sense that Chaucer was the poet his culture particularly
needed to rediscover at that point in its history, out of a sense of mission,

the resulting translations would have been lesser works, equivalents of the 'opinion-forming' pieces written by today's ubiquitous 'cultural commentators'. Like translators, critics engaged in acts of memorial need to maintain some perplexity as to what it is which is most to be commemorated about the author they commemorate. *John Dryden: Tercentenary Essays* is not in this salutary muddle. Its contributors are too rarely at cross-purposes with each other, so that the picture of Dryden which emerges from the volume as a whole is too much of a whole, too firm in its outlines to seem a fair likeness of a poet who said of himself, as Paul Hammond's introduction reminds us Dryden did, 'As I am a Man, I must be changeable.' In the first instance, the feeling that the volume does not do justice to the celebrated (or, by his enemies, castigated) variousness of Dryden's work arises from the narrow gauge it takes of that work, evident not only at the level of genre (as I said earlier) but also of chronology – nine of the essays treat works Dryden wrote in the last seven of his fifty years as a writer, leaving only three to cover the first forty-three. But underlying that restricted span of attention is a deeper community of purpose, which, though it might gladden the heart of a publisher, may bode less well for the future of Dryden scholarship: a determination to rescue Dryden from the 'comparative neglect ... by our best critics and brightest students' which 'has led to him now being the least appreciated of our great poets', to win for him a new generation of readers. This is a good intention, one which should be shared by any lover and teacher of Dryden, and yet, like other such intentions, it may not lead us quite to the destination we had in mind. Commentators who set out to write about Dryden in order to restore him to his rightful eminence may be on the road not to renewing interest in his works among modern readers, but to reforming him into the sort of poet such readers may find 'worth receiving'.

There are signs of this beginning to happen in *John Dryden: Tercentenary Essays*. The volume's of-the-moment-ness is most apparent in Steven Zwicker's 'Dryden and the Dissolution of Things: The Decay of Structures in Dryden's Later Writing', which detects a millenial atmosphere in *Fables*, while others of the essays train our gaze away from those phases and features of Dryden's writing which might seem alien or rebarbative, difficult to accommodate to modern expectations, and onto aspects of his temperament and career which are more amenable to those expectations. Hence, for instance, Paulina Kewes's relation of *Aureng-Zebe* to that most current of historiographical preoccupations, the formation of a 'public sphere' in seventeenth-century England; and hence, most significantly, the sustained assault throughout the volume on the idea that Dryden epitomized 'Augustan' literary values, an assault launched by Harold Love, whose 'Constructing Classicism: Dryden and Purcell' argues that 'despite his veneration for the Roman Augustan poets, his creative allegiances were at least as strongly to the silver age as to the golden', indeed that 'his strongest artistic debt as a young man was to native and Continental Mannerism'; and supported by Tom Mason and Adam Rounce, by Cedric Reverand, and by James Winn, who dwell severally on forms of anti-Augustanism in Dryden, the sublime intensity of *Alexander's Feast*, his self-identification in later years with an 'amoral, manipulative' conception of the poet, and the passionate excesses of his Homeric style.

Considered individually, these essays are cogently argued and persuasive; but, in the absence of any counter-balancing discussion of those aspects of Dryden's disposition and work which originally led to his being thought of as 'Augustan', in particular his lifelong commitment as a critic and a poet to Virgil, their cumulative effect is to imply that such a view of him is flatly wrong, and that the previous generation of readers of Dryden who held it were absolutely misguided. Literary history, like other kinds of history, does not work like this, is not so unambiguous a narrative of progress, as Dryden himself repeatedly insisted – one of the 'defamiliarizing challenges' his work presents to modern expectations is its consistent mistrust of advocates of 'reformation', whether in literary criticism or in religion or in politics. On the evidence of *John Dryden: Tercentenary Essays*, the challenge which confronts admirers of the poet on the three-hundredth anniversary of his death is to bring the proto-Romantic qualities of Dryden's writing, which these essays restore, into relation with his commitment to classical ideals of poise and propriety, a commitment less congenial to twenty-first-century tastes and no doubt exaggerated by past commentators, but without which Dryden is not Dryden. In the republic of letters, as in the political commonwealth of *Absalom and Achitophel*,

> If ancient fabrics nod, and threat to fall,
> To patch the flaws and buttress the wall
> Thus far 'tis duty ...

But 'innovation' is often 'the blow of fate', and 'To change foundations, and cast the frame anew' may be to 'mend the parts by ruin of the whole'.

John Dryden:
The Living and the Dead

Tom Mason

Dryden and the Traces of Classical Rome. By Paul Hammond. Pp. xii+305. Oxford: Oxford University Press, 1999. Hb. £45.

The Just and the Lively: The Literary Criticism of John Dryden. By Michael Werth Gelber. Pp. 342. Manchester: Manchester University Press, 1999. Hb. £40.

> I trade both with the Living and the Dead, for the enrichment of our Native Language.
>
> – Dryden, *Dedication of the Æneis* (1698)

> As a Translator he was just; as an Inventor he was rich. His Versions of some parts of Lucretius, Horace, Homer, and Virgil throughout, give him a just pretence to that Compliment which was made to Monsieur d'Ablancourt, a celebrated French Translator; It is uncertain who have the greatest Obligations to Him, the Dead or the Living.
>
> – Samuel Garth, *Dedication* to *Ovid's Metamorphoses* (1717)

It is not easy to assess Dryden's standing in the professional mind or among non-professional readers (if there are any such) at the beginning of a new century – whether as a poet, as a translator, as a critic, or in general. Some popular accounts (that given on *Britannica Online*, for example) imply that Dryden's reputation has never been higher. It might be hard to support such a suggestion; it both is and is not correct. On the one hand, one might point to the fact that Dryden's life has been more fully documented and his works better edited than at any time in the past. Those writing professionally seem to consider it unnecessary to apologize for their author as much or as often as used to be the case. Some may even have the impression that Dryden's position as the most profound and various of all poetic translators is assured. On the other hand, and at the same time, the rest of the world goes about its business regardless. For many students both of Latin and of English literature,

Dryden's is a difficult idiom, his critical positions beyond sympathy. When undergraduate courses and anthologies are squeezed, it tends to be Dryden's poems that go to the wall. In some recent anthologies, Dryden appears to have dwindled to a shadow deep in the background to Aphra Behn.

Both these books attempt to take Dryden very seriously indeed. And both, in apparently opposite ways, attempt to address the problem of Dryden's disregard. Gelber, believing that Dryden's criticism belongs with the living, presents it as a refuge from various 'modernisms' to which English critics might turn in 'moments of despondency' when they 'begin to feel that all is not well in the republic of letters'. The necessary corrective is Dryden's 'insistence that English literature, as an expression of national character and genius, fulfils itself by combining somehow the just with the lively'. The Preface to *Fables*, for example, 'bears the whole stamp' of Dryden's 'personality and genius', and, Gelber argues, in that it is 'easygoing but self-confident, good-humoured and firm, learned but graceful, stunning in its flexibility, exhilarating in its intelligence and good sense', is 'the kind of essay or criticism which, in the present age, our structuralists, deconstructionists, post-structuralists, hermeneuticists, and semioticians would do well to read and study and take to heart'.

Hammond, in marked contrast, deploys a vocabulary that draws quiet attention to a common ground between (some of) Dryden's concerns and (some of) those of (some) modern theory. His invitation is to entertain a vocabulary derived from Derrida (*'différance'*, *'sous-rasure'*) and to follow 'traces' distinctly different from, and yet continuous with, the 'tracks' of Ben Jonson which Dryden in *Of Dramatic Poesie* had described as found everywhere in the 'snow' of Latin poets. Dryden's translations produce, or exist in, a 'macaronic space' where his own thoughts are both reshaped and diverted:

> Language carries within it the traces of its past, quasi-archaeological remains from structures of thought which have crumbled away; and literary language, with its heightened self-consciousness, is especially aware of the origins from which its present culture springs, or claims to spring. To write is to be engaged in a passionate relation to the origin.

Both writers present Dryden as thoughtful, intelligent, and engaged – but in both cases that thought, engagement, and intelligence is (properly and inevitably) presented as a specialized thing – the appreciation of which is the reward for hard and sustained study. And yet both Gelber and Hammond write with infectious enthusiasm. Gelber's love of his subject is open and avowed. Hammond's passion slips out in the intersections of his sober and careful discussion, which is, however, always passionately sober and enthusiastically careful. Both writers are steeped in Dryden's works (although some readers may think that Gelber too rarely turns from Dryden's critical remarks to the poems and plays they discuss or introduce). Hammond, in particular, writes with the authority of an editor – one who has considered every word in every one of Dryden's poems in relation to every other word, and in relation to every source and every commentary on that source.

Will either book affect Dryden's standing in the world? Gelber, despite endorsement of Steven Zwicker, is likely to be dismissed as *démodé*. Hammond's book is perhaps of most value to the already converted. His discussion of Dryden's wide and profound interests as revealed by or expressed in the translations is always subtle, and, after due consideration, persuasive. The case made for the intelligence, subtlety, and thoughtfulness of Dryden's translations is overwhelming, but may have greater appeal to the Restoration specialist than the reader whose first interests are in the Latin authors Dryden translated, or the reader whose interests lie even slightly to one side. And his book does not, perhaps, provide many reasons why the non-specialist might want to bother in the first place. Hammond's Dryden, that is, might seem to give support to those who argue that every age produces its own translations, which mirror that age, and the interest of which, therefore, pertains exclusively to that age.

But perhaps this is to over-simplify Hammond's argument:

> What Dryden creates, in effect, is a translation which is a double-faced but not duplicitous commentary, a text folded at once towards its Latin original and towards its origin in Restoration culture. On the one side, Dryden's text explains obscurities and specific historical details in the Latin by including brief glosses within the text of the translation rather than in notes; on the other side, in its second field, it turns the original poems towards late seventeenth-century England as a mirror for the times, a commentary on the needs and follies of the age.

Here the virtues of the editor produce concomitant limitations. There may appear to be a gap between the Dryden who addressed the preoccupations of 'the seventeenth-century mind' and the Dryden who appealed or might appeal to later readers. Implicitly, the modern reader is assumed – or encouraged – to possess or to develop peculiarly late-seventeenth-century interests, to read as if living in the closing years of that century. So Hammond writes that some of the 'startling' 'cross-cuts' between the Roman and the modern worlds 'remind us that we, as Restoration Englishmen, have failed to inherit Roman simplicity and virtue, however much we may proclaim our interest in the Roman cultural heritage'. The assumption at such moments is that, in order to become proper readers of Dryden's translations, 'we' have somehow to become Restoration Englishmen, or rather, that attending to Dryden's poems necessarily turns us into Restoration Englishmen – and for Restoration Englishmen, it is assumed, political concerns were likely to be paramount. Despite the carefulness and scrupulousness of the discussion, and several contrary arguments, a reader may come away from Hammond's book with the impression that, particularly in the translations from Virgil, Dryden's reasons for translating and the interest of the translation itself were, are, and will be primarily political: 'He was making his own poem in part a distillation of earlier versions: a rendering which registered the form and pressure of his own age, while directing the reader to other ways of thinking.'

For many readers this emphasis is likely to provide some of the principal attractions of Hammond's book – since it seems to be the case that the political events surrounding Dryden's life and works are of peculiarly pressing interest to some modern scholars. And it is no doubt both necessary and desirable that every serious reader of Dryden should allow *part* of the mind to recreate an imagined past susceptibility, including past political sensitivities. Every one of Dryden's translations, it would be uncontentious to say, bears some relation to its immediate history. The language of the poem achieves a peculiar resonance in relation to that immediate history. But that is, perhaps, only the beginning of the story. The reasons for reading the poems with such an effort of historical imagination in the first place probably depend on other aspects of the mind and other aspects of the poems. If Dryden had not turned his engagement with Latin authors into poetry which interested later generations with altered concerns, there would be no reason to pay his translations more sustained attention than is given to, say, those of Thomas Creech.

While it is always worth drawing attention to the intelligence of Dryden's translations, an intelligence that showed not least in his own awareness of the similarities and dissimilarities between the politics of Augustan Rome and those of seventeenth-century England, it might be worth stressing that his purposes were often larger than to please his immediate audience – or that his immediate audience considered poetry to be a mode of writing that was likely to interest generations yet unborn.

(In the Preface to the *Fables* Dryden entertains the possibility that his works might last as long as Chaucer's had done, or be revived as Chaucer's had been.) An ideal reader of Dryden's translations needs, perhaps, to become an eighteenth-century, or nineteenth-century, reader, as well as one who belongs to the Restoration (and to the twenty-first century)

One such later reader, notable for his absence in Hammond's book, might be Samuel Johnson. In the fifty-eighth number of the *Adventurer* Johnson presents two explanatory readings of Horace. These are offered as insights for which readers might be grateful. Part of his argument, however, looks in the opposite direction:

> It often happens, that an author's reputation is endangered in
> · succeeding times, by that which raised the loudest applause among
> his cotemporaries: nothing is read with greater pleasure than
> allusions to recent facts, reigning opinions, or present
> controversies; but when facts are forgotten, and controversies
> extinguished, these favourite touches lose all their grace; and the
> author in his descent to posterity must be left to the mercy of
> chance, without any power of ascertaining the memory of those
> things, to which he owed his luckiest thoughts, and his kindest
> reception.

Johnson several times points out that the immediate reasons for the success of a work may become, with time, impediments to pleasure. As Gelber argues, Johnson's account of the literary-historical importance of Dryden's work derives from Dryden's own account of himself, and is itself a testimony to the persisting life of Dryden's critical thought. Of the discussion of the principles of translation outlined by Dryden in the 'Preface to Ovid's *Epistles*', Gelber points out that 'Johnson makes it perfectly clear that without qualification he accepts the theory, the whole of it, and that he cannot but admire Dryden for both his learning and his common sense.' (Gelber also draws attention to Johnson's use of a large range of Dryden's writing about translation – including Dryden's remarks on Cowley, Holiday, and Sandys.) For Johnson it is the mark of great poetry, like that of Shakespeare, for example, to survive a loss of immediate interest. Dryden's power of pleasing, in his translations and elsewhere, was not, for Johnson, dependent on his allusion to recent fact, reigning opinions, or present controversy. If Dryden is the poet who taught us 'the bounds of a translator's liberty', Johnson's praise of Dryden's translations themselves is grounded on their simple power to please, that power which, 'in opposition to reason, makes Ariosto the darling and the pride of Italy', and which, 'in defiance of criticism, continues Shakespeare the sovereign of the drama':

> Works of imagination excel by their allurement and delight; by their power of attracting and detaining the attention. That book is good in vain which the reader throws away. He only is the master who keeps the mind in pleasing captivity; whose pages are perused with eagerness, and in hope of new pleasure are perused again; and whose conclusion is perceived with an eye of sorrow, such as the traveller casts upon departing day.
>
> (*Lives*, I, 453–4)

That book is good in vain that the reader throws away. How did Dryden's *Æneis* – along with many of his translations of other authors – survive the generation that saw its publication? As Johnson saw it, weak competition had been offered to Dryden's Virgil by Joseph Trapp (1679–1747) in *The Works of Virgil: Translated into English Blank Verse* (1731), and challenging competition by Christopher Pitt (1699–1748) in *The Works of Virgil, in Latin and English* (1753). In his 'Life', Johnson describes Pitt as 'engaging as a rival with Dryden', as having 'observed his failures, and avoided them', and, imitating Pope's *Iliad*, as having employed 'an exact, equable, and splendid versification'. What were the qualities that allowed Dryden's version to recover its place in popular estimation? Johnson's answer was that 'Dryden leads the reader forward by his general vigour and sprightliness' while 'Pitt often stops him to contemplate the excellence of a single couplet': 'Dryden's faults are forgotten in the hurry of delight, and … Pitt's beauties are neglected in the languor of a cold and listless perusal; … Pitt pleases the criticks, and Dryden the people; … Pitt is quoted, and Dryden read' (*Lives*, III, 279–80).

Some of the most interesting pages in Hammond's book discuss the episode in the second Book of the *Æneis* when Pyrrhus kills Polites, one of Priam's sons, full in the sight of his father, and then kills the old king himself. Although, as Johnson makes clear, there are difficulties in comparing isolated passages, this episode may serve as a representative test case. Johnson's key terms – 'general vigour' and 'sprightliness', 'the hurry of delight' – are perhaps not very helpful to a modern reader, but a case for the liveliness of Dryden's version might be supported by his attention to the details of the scene – as when describing the feeble flight of the old king's spear, which Dryden (742–5) appears to have wanted his readers to see and hear:

> This said, his feeble hand a Javelin threw,
> Which flutt'ring, seem'd to loiter as it flew:
> Just, and but barely, to the Mark it held,
> And faintly tinkl'd on the Brazen Shield.

(while Trapp concentrates attention rather on the end of the spear's flight as it hangs from Pyrrhus' shield –

> So spake the aged Sire; And feebly flung,
> Without a Wound, an unperforming Dart:
> Which, by the Target's sounding Brass repuls'd,
> Hung on the Surface of it's bossy Orb.

– and Pitt seems to follow Dryden, but with more effort than force:

> This said, his trembling arm essay'd to throw
> The dull dead javelin, that scarce reach'd the foe;
> The weapon languishingly lagg'd along,
> And, guiltless, on the buckler faintly rung.)

Dryden's attention to detail appears to be subserving larger ends. In the speech that precedes the throwing of the spear, Dryden, in contrast to the later translators, seems concerned to present this moment as one overtly designed to be of permanent interest to humankind. His version makes 'Nature's Law' both the motive force for Priam's words and their subject. Dryden's Priam claims that Achilles obeyed these laws, while Pyrrhus is placed (by poet and king) as beyond them – outside them, or beneath them. When Priam saw Polites 'gasping at his feet',

> The Fear of death gave place to Nature's Law.
> And shaking more with Anger, than with Age,
> The Gods, said He, requite thy brutal Rage:
> As sure they will, Barbarian, sure they must,
> If there be Gods in Heav'n, and Gods be just:
> Who tak'st in Wrongs an insolent delight;
> With a Son's death t'infect a Father's sight.
> Not He, whom thou and lying Fame conspire
> To call thee his; Not He, thy vaunted Sire,
> Thus us'd my wretched Age: The Gods he fear'd,
> The Laws of Nature and of Nations heard.
> He chear'd my Sorrows, and for Sums of Gold,
> The bloodless Carcass of my *Hector* sold:

Pity'd the Woes a Parent underwent,
And sent me back in safety from his Tent.

(727–41)

Hammond notes that Dryden, when describing the death of Priam, has
added several important details to Virgil: the shade is 'violated'; the king
is a 'Royal Victim'; the sword-thrust goes to the Priam's heart; the blood
gushes from the wound and stains the 'sacred ground'. Hammond also
suggests that the line 'A headless Carcass, and a nameless thing'
represents Dryden as recoiling from the death of Priam, in that it is
taken verbatim from Sir John Denham's translation in *The Destruction of
Troy*, occasioning Dryden's only footnote to the poem. In this case
Pitt's version (given next) appears to emulate Dryden's (immediately
following):

> Thou then be first, replies the chief, to go
> With these sad tidings to his ghost below;
> Begone—acquaint him with my crimes in Troy,
> And tell my sire of his degenerate boy.
> Die then: he said, and dragg'd the monarch on,
> Thro' the warm blood that issu'd from his son,
> Stagg'ring and sliding in the slipp'ry gore,
> And to the shrine the royal victim bore;
> Lock'd in the left he grasps the silver hairs,
> High in the right the flaming blade he rears,
> Then to the hilt with all his force apply'd,
> He plung'd the ruthless fau'chion in his side.
> Such was the fate unhappy Priam found,
> Who saw his Troy lie levell'd with the ground;
> He, who round Asia sent his high commands,
> And stretch'd his empire o'er a hundred lands;
> Now lies a headless carcass on the shore,
> The man, the monarch, and the name no more!

> Then *Pyrrhus* thus: Go thou from me to Fate;
> And to my Father my foul deeds relate.
> Now dye. With that he dragg'd the trembling Sire,
> Slidd'ring through clotter'd Blood, and holy Mire,
> (The mingl'd Paste his murder'd Son had made,) ⎫
> Haul'd from beneath the violated Shade; ⎬
> And on the Sacred Pile, the Royal Victim laid. ⎭
> His right Hand held his bloody Faulchion bare;

His left he twisted in his hoary Hair:
Then, with a speeding Thrust, his Heart he found: ⎫
The lukewarm Blood came rushing through the wound, ⎬
And sanguine Streams distain'd the sacred Ground. ⎭
Thus *Priam* fell: and shar'd one common Fate
With *Troy* in Ashes, and his ruin'd State:
He, who the Scepter of all *Asia* sway'd,
Whom Monarchs like domestick Slaves obey'd.
On the bleak Shoar now lies th' abandoned King,
A headless Carcass, and a nameless thing.

(746–63)

Hammond points out that the word 'slidd'ring' is used nowhere else in Dryden's verse, not being recorded by the *OED* in the previous two centuries, and that 'clotter'd (as a variant form of 'clotted') seems to have been archaic by Dryden's day, and was perhaps borrowed from Chapman. Dryden's 'special horror', argues Hammond, is 'signalled by his departure from Virgil's linguistic sobriety'. Dryden's expression or representation of horror in the word 'slidd'ring', it might be added, appears to be one minute example of his enrichment of the language. As was often his practice, Alexander Pope remembered, amplified, and animated Dryden's departure from conventional decorum – in this case when he came to the moment in *Iliad* XXI (Pope's 264–7) when Achilles fights with the river Scamander, a passage Pope found to display 'a great Beauty in the Versification':

The falling Deluge whelms the Hero round:
His loaded Shield bends to the rushing Tide;
His Feet, upborn, scarce the strong Flood divide,
Slidd'ring, and stagg'ring.

From Pope, the word (together with Pope's addition) was returned by Pitt to Virgil and to Pyrrhus: 'Stagg'ring and sliding in the slipp'ry gore'. Such employment of Dryden's vocabulary by Pope and Pitt represents a tiny example of Dryden's impressing later readers by a very particular 'vigour and sprightliness'.

   Gelber points out that Johnson's account of the general literary-historical importance of Dryden derives from Dryden's own account of himself in the 'Postscript to the Reader' attached to his *Æneis*:

For, what I have done, Imperfect as it is, for want of Health and leisure to Correct it, will be judg'd in after Ages, and possibly in

the present, to be no dishonour to my Native Country ...
Somewhat (give me leave to say) I have added to both of them in
the choice of Words, and Harmony of Numbers which were
wanting, especially the last, in all our Poets, even in those who
being endu'd with Genius, yet have not Cultivated their Mother-
Tongue with sufficient Care; or relying on the Beauty of their
Thoughts, have judg'd the Ornaments of Words, and sweetness of
Sound unnecessary.

Gelber observes that 'Dryden takes up three subjects ("'Words",
"Numbers", "Thoughts") and makes claims for himself in just two', and
that 'with a slight change in vocabulary ("Language" for "Words",
"sentiments" for "Thoughts"), Johnson takes up the same subjects and
advances claims for Dryden in all three'. Johnson wrote:

> the veneration with which his name is pronounced by every
> cultivator of English literature is paid to him as he refined the
> language, improved the sentiments, and tuned the numbers of
> English Poetry.
>
> (*Lives*, I, 419)

The sentiments that Dryden 'improved' do not seem to have been of
peculiar interest to 'the Restoration Reader'. Nevertheless, if Dryden's
translations from Virgil are ever to carry away twenty-first century
readers in a 'hurry of delight', it is very much to be wished that the
Longman edition of Dryden, so subtly and illuminatingly edited by Paul
Hammond and David Hopkins, should be extended to include Dryden's
Æneis – together with the just and lively criticism that accompanies it.

Index